BETWEEN A ROCK & A HOLY PLACE

For my dear Jackie
I love you dearly
and
thank God for sharing
you with me ! ♡
Donna

TABLE OF CONTENTS

a note from the author

05   when you walk into a room

15   mr. and mrs. goose

27   do Lord... do remember me

39   she dances

49   winter trees & dandelions

57   with paper dolls in a cardboard box

63   have courage, be kind

73   three perfectly timed words

79   changing my focus & thinking of you

87   finding a new way in an old wave

103   joy is a choice

113   behind the veil

123   was she found with her hands wide open?

133   fishing for life

143   elephants and a boy, salt and light

151   oh the places He is found

163   between a rock & a holy place

171   a little about the author

175   book preview: Dandelion

CONTENT GUIDE

PRAYER   113 | 151

LOVE   01 | 15 | 57 | 63 | 73 | 79 | 113

COURAGE   15 | 49 | 63 | 73

JOY   39 | 103 | 133

SURRENDER   27 | 39 | 49 | 57 | 79 | 87 | 103
123 | 133 | 143 | 151 | 163

FAITH   27 | 39 | 103 | 123 | 143 | 163

a note from the author

Someone, somewhere long ago coined the phrase, "Between a rock and a hard place." And while this book title has a play on those words, its meaning is altogether different. Allow me to explain. When someone finds themselves between a rock and a hard place, whatever choice they make is going to be difficult. There will be no easy, simple, or comfortable solution to the problem in front of them. We've all been in those places. Some of us more than others. When we first moved to Kenya I was often found in that most unsettling place of "this is going to be hard".

When stepping from the normal-ness of one place into the foreign-ness of another, there are bumps along the way. Easy and comfortable was not an option. Between a rock and a hard place became a new normal. I struggled. It wasn't pretty. But it was fruitful. One morning during my daily crying-out to the Lord, the words came to my heart, "You're missing the holy-ness that's found in the hard places." What? I sat with those words for days. I wrote them down. I argued with them. I debated possible options of leaving the hard places completely. But I knew, there was a portion of gold that could be found in the settling-in of the simple truth. Would I allow it to come? When obedience and disobedience are the only two options, I fear. It's a good kind of fear, since it's all laced with God Himself. I fear disobeying the One who holds the ground under my feet and the stars above and gives me breath and heart-beat. It's an in-awe-of sort of fear and it's good for the soul. Disobedience just isn't an option when our eyes are set on the Mountain Maker. Like who would stand in front of the KING and say, "no"? Courage on the battlefield requires humility first in front of the King.

So, after a bit of struggling and a river of tears, I let the right words sink in. I began viewing my new world as an opportunity to see more God-moments in the Holy places rather than feel over-whelmed by the hard places. I quit longing for soft and easy, instead I watched for Him and followed His lead. It's the beginnings of the grandest of adventures and most challenging moments, but is there any better way to use air? If we consider that we have maybe 80 years of life, and if the average person breaths 20 breaths each minute of that life, then we can loosely deduce that each of us has been given the gift of about 840,960,000 breaths to breathe. Look at that! You're a millionaire after all!

Someone might say a breath is different than a dollar, and they would be right. But without a breath you die; without a dollar you can still find a way. So from that perspective, I ask, which is more valuable? I'm going with breathing. And since I've been given the enormous gift of a millionaire's portion of air, I want to use it well.

Being a good steward of my breathes is my responsibility. (Just as being a good steward of every dollar is as well.) It was in these deep-thinking moments God spoke to my heart in defining-moment ways. In a whisper He conveyed to my tear-soaked heart, *"Life is hard Donna, I told you it would be in John 16:33b. 'In this world you will have trouble. But take heart! I have overcome the world.' So could we just get past that fact and let's do hard together. I'll be with you. You are not alone. And I know the way that's best for you. Will you trust me? Life will bring the hard, but if you'll let Me, I will bring the HOLY. You won't feel stuck between a rock and a hard place, instead, you'll feel My holiness in those rock-hard places. Remember, I AM the Rock where you can stand. So let hard become the place you seek Holy and we will do life together. Breathe air beside Me."*

So I decided to try this way of living like a millionaire beside the Good One. I hope this book encourages you in a way that compels you to join me in choosing to live like a millionaire between a rock and a Holy Place.

With so much love in every breath,
Donna

ONE

when you walk into a room

When you walk into a room, what happens? How does your arrival make others *feel*? Are they intimidated? Happy? Anxious?

When we walk into a room, sometimes, no one notices. But more often than we realize, others will have a subtle emotion surge through them when we enter. How we live beside them, how we respond to them, how we look at them begins to author the emotion they feel. Are we a calming influence? Do they feel rejected? Can they feel safe? Do we make them feel insecure?

Jesus showed us the importance of seeing others and responding to them in right ways. When Jesus walked into a room, things changed. And when He left this earth, He said we would do all He had done — and more.

So, i've been sitting with a question. What happens when I walk into a room? Do joy and peace arrive with me? Or do I bring anxiety and strife? Something more than just flesh and bones enters when we walk into a room. Something more than used air will remain after we go. If we asked 10 people closest to us to share one word describing how our presence makes them feel, what words would they use?

Wherever we go, we fill up that space with more than can be seen. When we walk out of a room, we leave something behind. People feel better, worse, or completely untouched. Have we warmed hearts or chilled them? It's the precursor to the legacy we will leave when we die.

It's what Heaven's been whispering to me of late.

———————

On a Monday we prayed again over my aching chest. The cough had first come four weeks earlier. Tears had dominated my night; fear is a mean bedfellow. Ugly thoughts like, "could this be the beginnings of a heart attack?" Since i've never had one, how can I know how it would feel? I'mnot typically a worrier, but this extended sickness had begun to win and I was losing the battle in my mind. After lots of prayer, and sorting out many details, my husband bought the ticket to fly me home the next day. It's the cheapest ticket we've ever bought between Kenya and home, what a relief.

Tuesday I boarded the plane. Twenty-three hours later I landed in

Atlanta. People surrounded me. But my eyes searched only for my daughter. Maggie walked into the room at the international arrivals in Atlanta — everything changed. A sparkle of *home* arrived with her. Flowers in hand, she brought peace, calm, love, and the sense of you-are-not-alone. It all walked in the room with her. My chest still ached, but my heart breathed more easily.

The next day found me sitting in a doctor's office. Friends had made the appointment for me, we'd spoken with them just minutes after booking my flight on Monday. I needed to see a doctor, they made the arrangements for me (thank you Gene and Jackie!). Seventy-two hours later found me in his office. I sat quietly on the high examination table, Jackie and I watched the door. The doctor would soon arrive; he would bring a knowledge of what was wrong with my chest and what needed to be done. The doorknob turned, Dr. Momin walked in, a smile and a greeting, and I knew answers would soon come.

When the doctor walked into the room — everything changed. Before meds were even prescribed, my thoughts shifted and I felt better, just knowing someone was present who knew what to do. No more guessing, I could rest. It was only bronchitis and pleurisy. The words heart attack or lung disease never came. It's a tiring battle to keep believing the best when your mind runs rampant over less appealing possibilities. When someone who could give an educated answer walked into the room, there was no more space for battlegrounds in my mind.

Two days later I sat in a room proportionate to a castle hall. Called the "Great Room", it a quiet space where students can retreat from the continuous activity of university life. My youngest son had said, "Mom, while you're home, come to class with me." He now attends my alma mater. It's a beautiful campus in a small gold mining town, hence the steeple on the oldest building is covered in gold found in the mines long ago. Between classes we walked pathways familiar to us both. I shared stories of the places his father and I had sat and talked during our dating days, before a wedding ring, before children. Under the same-same oak trees, walking the same-same pathways, my son now journeys where I once did, and we felt time shrink.

As class called him away, I headed to the great room, he would meet me there after lectures were done. It's a dark room with a stained glass window on one end, flags hanging high around two perimeter walls, and couches neatly placed in groupings. I chose my spot, slid off my sandals, curled up against the cushions and studied along with the other much-younger-students in the great room. They delved into books like physics and foreign language, poli sci and calculus. I opened familiar pages of ancient history laced with endless love. My Bible, my greatest study, my home.

I read, journaled, read more, prayed. Mentally sitting right beside the hems of His robe, and wiped tears over the flood that came. The hour flew by. Looking up from my studies, I saw him round the corner. Peter walked into the room — everything changed. There came that smile on his face as he found me in the dark great room, that smile of recognition, that look that silently says, "There you are, I know you, i've been looking for you." Familiar kindness, peace, calm... it all came into the room with him.

Days later, I sat in my parents beautiful mountain home. It's their weekend runaway, where the deer battle with my mother over her newly planted flowers and the trees wrestle with my dad over their leafy covering of his long mountain views. It's a place of silence and peace even with these playful wrestlings of nature. Mom and Dad know, the mountain owns itself really (the Deed in their hands means nothing to the mountain), and the trees and deer and bear see their lovely home as a well manicured playground. We'd laughed the night before as we stayed up late and talked.

Early morning found me perched in the quaint sitting room off their breakfast area, holding leather-bound-home in my hands again and talking with the One. Everywhere can be home with Him. Finishing up my readings, I sat quiet. The morning sun was shaking the shoulders of the mountains as a mother does the shoulders of her children, "time to wake up." Light leaked into the little room wrapped in windows. Then a sleepy mom and dad walked into the room — everything changed. Familiar flooded in. Familiar faces with familiar voices, for over five decades. Safety, kindness and I-miss-seeing-your-face walked in with them.

My short two week visit home was a flood of much-needed-moments with those dear to me--- walking into the room. And for those two weeks, I allowed myself the gift. Mentally, I wrapped each entry as if it were a literal present. It was an unplanned trip. A last minute decision. "Go home to see a doctor" (chest pains pressed the decision), but also, and perhaps even more important, go home to see your children, your family, rest in quiet places with souls that your heart is aching to see. Perhaps it wasn't pleurisy that pressed me home after all... no, it wasn't a heart attack... instead it was a heart in need. My dear husband gave me this gift, "Go spend Mother's day early with them. The time it will take to fly there and back will be about the same amount of hours you labored to bring them into this world." What a thought.

As I flew back to Kenya, sitting alone surrounded by people, I revisited all the moments of familiar faces walking into the room. Words are not able to share the heart sometimes.

It's perhaps one of the great griefs of releasing a loved one to the grave. The pain of knowing they will never walk into the room again. Living so far from home, I do think on such things. And it grows me. Others-centered thoughts, not self-centered ones. Appreciating the fact that when someone walks into a room with us — it is a gift that will not be allowed always. This should not provoke sadness; this should provoke appreciation. See the soul that enters the room. Embrace the gift that has come near, and go a step further still. Ask ourselves to be truthful about what others might feel when we walk into their rooms.

In the blink of an eye, my visit was over. Good meds had defeating the chest pains and coughing. I'd rested near my children in my daughter and son-in-law's home. Getting to lay my head down under a roof that's also covering the heads of those I gave birth to, well that's better than ten Christmas mornings for me.

Waiting on airport tarmac, anticipating those wheels leaving home-soil again. Those moments of seeing them *walk into the room* filled in the cracked pain of leaving them again.

Landing back in Kenya, I held that same leather-bound-home in my hands. And I purposed in my heart to appreciate who would be walking into the room here. My Steve. We who have been married for many years can all too often overlook the gift that should be seen when they walk into the room. Steve and I have been married for almost four decades, that's over 14,000 days of walking in to each others rooms. Too many let it become common — it should not be.

Walking into the room. It was a thought, a grouping of words that I'd been studying on for nearly two weeks. How it felt when others walked into my room, how it might have felt for them when I walked into theirs.

Then two days after my return home to Kenya, I sat with a mission-ary friend as we prepared to lead worship on Sunday. She had chosen several songs for us to consider. She played her guitar, we sang. Coming to a song I'd never heard before, she sang it alone while I closed my eyes and listened. She sang the words, "When You walk into the room, everything changes..." She did not know the journey I'd been on with those very words. I opened my eyes and reached for the song sheet, as she continued to sing. "When You walk into the room, everything changes. Darkness starts tremble at the light that You bring. When You walk into the room, every heart starts burning and nothing matters more than just to sit here at Your feet and worship You."

When Maggie walked into the airport arrivals room,
everything changed for me.

When the doctor walked into the examination room,
everything changed.

When Peter walked into the great room at university,
everything changed for me.

When my parents walked into the quiet-time room,
everything changed.

When I walked back into the room with my Steve,
everything changed for me.

There were countless other moments of special room arrivals, each of which is dear... and perhaps I appreciate them all the more because it is not often I get to see them walk into my rooms.

But when it came in a song, "When you walk into the room, everything changes, darkness starts to tremble at the Light that You bring..." Heaven whispered. He had been giving me glimpses of it – the importance of what happens when love walks into a room.

Truth — when we walk into each other's rooms, it matters. We bring something with us when we arrive. We bring joy or angst, peace or turmoil. And we actually get to choose. We should choose well what we allow to enter a room with us. It will matter, more than we know.

Heart-healing can come when others walk into our room. When the doctor walks in, when my children, my sister, my parents, my husband walk in. Heart-healing.

But soul-healing comes when He walks into our rooms. So when the room is filled with too much pain, too much lonely, too much ache, and we're longing for something to come and relieve the empty space around us, let's close our eyes and ask Him to walk into the room.

When He walks into the room — *everything* changes. We must not let the wild commotion and deep pains of life on planet earth keep us from remembering all we really need is for Him to walk into the room. And when we walk into the rooms of other's lives, we need to carry Him with us. Never forget, some of the most unkind among us have never *felt Him* walk into their aching rooms. May we carry Him all the more steadfastly into their hollow spaces.

TWO

mr. and mrs. goose

Yesterday I bought Ernest Hemingway's "The Snows of Kilmanjaro" for our oldest son. This morning I write sitting beside that mountain. Its snowy peak often hides behind the high clouds, hence its name, "the shy mountain".

In front of me is a sprinkling of much lesser mountains, they lay across the western side of Tsavo. Their peaks are too many to number and they're wrapped in acacia trees. They've been well watered this morning as rains came with the sunrise. But now, rainclouds have given way to blue and the trees sparkle, like cared for children in the cradle of these mountains.

Steve and Peter have gone for an early morning game drive. Usually I would be beside them, but my safari (journey) this morning will find me sitting still; opting to "be still" to think — pray — read — write. Rather than going to look for the animals, I will wait and see what comes to me.

The field in front of me is home to an Egyptian goose. Smaller than the rocks around it, it has captured my attention. How very "odd" I realize I have become. The giraffe mother and here babe have just disappeared back into the tall acacia, but it's the little goose who holds my rapt focus. Last night he peacefully sat alone beside the watering hole.

He weighs maybe 3 pounds soaking wet and his "hang" is a watering hole in Africa surrounded by animals that dwarf him in every way, and yet he moves about as if "all is well". Last night the zebra, who fear the darkness behind them, inched closer and closer to the watering hole. Mr. Goose glided out of the water, settled his webbed feet on the shoreline, and held his position without ruffling a feather. Did he not realize dozens of sharp hooves surrounded him and each held the power to end him? But almost as if he had been given the assignment to *be still* and *fear not* — that little goose silently preached to me, as I sat all comfy in my safari chair drinking tea (on the outside) and yet deep inside, I was squirming with discontentment and worry.

I know... I'mnot suppose to actually admit that am I? But sometimes I do wonder — who among us, wrapped in dust and clay, doesn't have their moments of trembling? If we did not know what trembling felt like, would we ever really reach for Abba's *be still and know that I AM GOD*?

Egyptian geese mate for life. They are rarely found alone. If you see one alone, then it is likely either eating while its mate roosts on their clutch of eggs or it hasn't found its life-mate yet. But for sure it will not rest until it finds the one it will live with for the rest of its days. A ranger once shared with us his great admiration of the feathery foul. He shared, "They will mate for life and they mean it. They are born with the need to be faithful to one and only one. They will live together for years and travel together always. On the day that one of them dies, the other will soon follow." We asked how that could be. He explained further, "On the day the male goose dies, the female will simply stop eating. She will slowly kill herself by starvation. But if the female dies first, the male will begin searching for her. Even if he sees her death, in disbelief he will fly to each of the many places they have nested over their years together. He will search for her. As he visits each place where she has been, and finds she is not there, he will fly on to the next place where he remembers being with her. When he has exhausted all possibilities, he makes one final flight, straight up. He beats wings hard to fly to the highest place he will ever go, then when he can ascend no further, he folds his wings for the last time and plummets to the ground below. It is his way of ending himself. He will not live without his she-goose."

The ranger ended by telling us how much he knew Kenyan men

could learn from the little goose. We knew he told us the story because he knew of our call to minister to marriages, but did he know how deeply the story moved us? And don't we all need to know of the faithful little goose? Husbands and wives everywhere need to realize there are feather-covered-faithful ones that sparkle with a goodness we skin-covered-souls often struggle to emulate.

Last night as I lay my head down, I pondered on the lone goose by the watering hole. He was the picture of what I should be. He was doing it so well. I found myself in class again. Time to learn from a wee feathered creature in a dangerous place.

My heart was engaged because — he was — alone. Egyptian geese are not suppose to be alone. It's instinctively placed inside them to have a companion, another goose — one goose —beside them. As I closed my eyes I wondered if he would still be by the muddy water in the morning. Imagine my lunacy as I thought to myself how I would like to go out to the water's edge, scoop him up in my arms, shower him off good, and let him be my little buddy for the rest of his days. He should not be alone... I would be his friend. (Surely Abba shakes His great head so often at me.)

This morning as I write, I smile for it is being proven to me, Mr. Goose was not alone after all. Mrs. Goose is right there beside him. They're walking about stirring up seeds and bugs, having their morning feast together. And even as I ponder over where she was last night, I watch as he waddles over to a hidden nest in a grassy mound, tucked carefully out of the way. It's nestled at the high edge of another watering hole where few animals would consider going. Smoother slopes are plentiful, where thirsty animals would more likely drink. The short escarpment edge is the perfect spot to grow their littles. Mr. Goose now sits, hidden, on the nest. Mrs. Goose is foraging about, appearing to be the lone goose now — but how thankful my heart is, to know she is not alone. They are together. They are working together. It's her turn to walk about and eat, while he tends their treasured eggs. And I'mreminded, he moved about during the more dangerous hours, when prey huddles near the watering hole and predators stretch muscles for a late night hunt.

He was not alone. She is not alone.
They know who they are and who they belong to and
what they are doing. And they do it.

The lilac-breasted roller glides into the acacia near by, with all its brilliant colors of blue and lavender, it moves about so freely and captures the attention of all who see its flight. What a beautiful bird. Mrs. Goose neither notices its glamorous arrival nor cares when it flies on. She doesn't ponder after its colorful flight, lamenting over her drab brown and grey plumage. She does not let her focus or her peace be intimidated by the flair of the other foul. She walks and eats, and holds faithful to the course before her. Just now she has paused to look up and to the right. She stares, something is in the bush and she watches. She eats nothing in these moments. She focuses closely. She's the very picture of confidence.

A goose can teach.

The movement in the bush ends (likely a mouse or lizard), she turns back to the ground. She doesn't fluster or fume, she's neither fearful nor irritated. She attends to her "calling". Graze and keep watch, then sit on the eggs and keep watch... graze and keep watch...sit on the eggs and keep watch.

A goose can teach.

Guinea fowl now approach her. She cares not. She doesn't run them off, selfishly gorging herself on the few seeds around her. She just peacefully continues eating. Guinea are adorable birds who look like little helmets running about in the open field. Hence their name, the helmeted guinea. With blue heads and a rounded body covered with white-polka-dotted black feathers, they run about comically. They are surely the most ADHD bird in Africa. They travel in flocks, many of them in a grouping. Does Mrs. Goose look at them and wonder, "Why can't I have more of my kind around me?" I watch her and I know the answer — she does not.

She is not a guinea fowl. She is a goose. She has an assignment in life, and if she ponders the guinea or the roller, it will only distract her from the faithful attention that is needed to be who she is and do what she is suppose to do. A goose, beside a muddy water hole in a dangerous place, can teach.

Do others think on the same sort of things? Or am I perhaps alone in my learning? There are those among us who are intensely l-o-n-e-l-y. Even surrounded by people, aloneness can still come. Some will distract themselves from the sense of aloneness by

a hobby	*something to do*
or work	*something to accomplish*
or buying	*something to have*
or going	*somewhere to be*
or watching	*something to entertain*
or medicating	*someway not to feel*
or drinking	*someway to numb*
or retreating	*someway to hide*
or succeeding	*someway to feel significant*
or dominating	*someway to feel powerful*
or denying	*someway to feel innocent*
or defending	*someway to feel right…*

it goes on and on.

Mr. and Mrs. Goose, they need none of this. They have a purpose, and they are sticking to it. No distractions are allowed. They know the frailty of life and the need for careful attention to the work they are called to. It's simple. It's sure. They won't change the world; they won't take from it. They will do their small part in it.

Brennan Manning seemed to be sitting at my table this morning, speaking ever so clearly with his writings in *Abba's Child*. He begins chapter eight with a powerfully blunt excerpt from Anthony DeMello's book *The Way to Love*.

DeMello writes:
"Look at your life and see how you have filled its emptiness with people. As a result they have a stranglehold on you. See how they control your behavior by their approval and disapproval. They hold the power to ease your loneliness with their company, to send your spirits soaring with their praise, to bring you down to the depths with their criticism and rejection. Take a look at yourself spending almost every waking moment of your day placating and pleasing people, whether they are living or dead.

"You live by their norms, conform to their standards, seek their company, desire their love, dread their ridicule, long for their applause, meekly submit to the guilt they lay upon you; you are terrified to go against the fashion in the way you dress or speak or act or even think. And observe how even when you control them you depend on them and are enslaved by them. People have become so much a part of your being that you cannot even imagine living a life that is unaffected or uncontrolled by them."

———————

I've read it over and over again. And... I think of Jesus, and how He does not fit inside the lines of that paragraph. He neither tried to control others nor did He allow others to have control over him. Instead, He was mastered only by His Father and because of that, He loved — perfectly. Ghandi's words echo again, "I like your Christ, I do not like your Christians. Your Christians are so unlike your Christ." Did Ghandi perhaps feel this way in part because we Christians so often look like DeMello's paragraph and our Christ looked/looks nothing like it.

Mrs. Goose was teaching this very lesson, better put, she was living this very way. Even as I write, I laugh at myself. Is it ludicrous to watch a couple of geese, consider how they live, and see something worth learning?

We might say, "…they are only geese, they do not have the pressures of human life imposed on them, they are born, they procreate, they survive until they die, and that is all there is for a goose. Human beings have so many more demands placed upon us."

But do we really?
Or do we impose so much more on ourselves?

Is it possible that the simple, focused, living of the geese by the watering hole, holds golden lessons we are too busy to notice? There are many differences for sure, but if we are wise, we will allow ourselves to learn from their silent sharing. And for today, as I seek to learn, I see this clearly. These geese are peaceful and gentle. If husbands and wives could interact as these geese do, there would be no broken homes with wounded children limping for years after the cave-in. They are focused on exactly what is their part:

— they graze and eat
— they stay near enough to help each other
— they are always watchful against those who would cause harm
— they are not concerned over what other birds think of them
— they don't criticize or judge other birds either
— they share what is around them and never complain
— they are thankful for another day of living, they know how close death is
— they never sleep too deeply nor celebrate to loudly (for they know there is always something lurking near)
— they don't compare themselves to others, and they don't tell other birds how they should behave.

They are focused, content, peaceful, persevering, dedicated.

In their solidarity and autonomy, they do not view their simple life as empty or lonely. They could... but they do not. As I watch the pair of simple geese, I rethink DeMello's words, and see that not one line applies to their life. Just as not one line of it applied to Jesus' life. When we think of Jesus's life, some might say, "well of course Jesus could live that way, after all, He is God in the form of man". So does that mean we don't press ourselves (as we should), to try and live like Him. But what can we say in defense of ourselves when we see two little geese living it well beside a watering hole in Africa? They are not controlled by the need to please or placate others. They do not crave the approval of others. They do not cringe over rejection of other feathery companions. They simply live well, according to the assignment they have been given in their lives. Perhaps we might say, "well, their assignment is simple..."

To this my heart hears this truth: *Our assignment is simple as well. In whatever we do, wherever we are found, in every moment we breathe another breath, we are called to one sure thing, we are to love others.*

There is a way to live focused, peaceful, content and faithful. Sharp hooves might surround us (unkind people saying unkind things, threatening to do even worse if they can). Hyenas might approach (those who look for death and then will devour us with bone crushing jaws that make us tremble). Feathered beauties might fly near (those who look, act, and sound perfect and who work to feel better about themselves as they compare their opulence to our simple walk). Or crowds of activity might swirl 'round us (when the life of others seems to be filled with "more" and we sit in our simplicity of "less").

But if we can keep our focus on "why" we are alive, then we too can make it through the dark nights by the watering holes. And the morning light will find us, doing what we were created to do: loving God and loving others.

Simple living that honors the One who made us, blesses those around us, and allows the one beside us to never feel alone (no matter how dark the night).

THREE

do Lord... do remember me

She sat still and sang loud, the little girl in Sunday School. The tune had a strong, easy flow. The kind of song that makes you feel like you're getting something done even sitting still. A tune that makes you smile from your toes up, and has a strength that lifts heaviness up and off weighed down shoulders... weighed down minds... weighed down hearts.

The teacher smiled as the children sang; singing in that uninhibited childhood abandon that doesn't worry what others might think or who might be critically watching the free flow of LIFE.

We grown ups worry though don't we? Some do.

We hold ourselves carefully, move not too much, clap when others clap, sit when others sit. We don't want to "distract" those around us, we wouldn't dare want our love flow towards the Lover of our Soul to *embarrass* anyone watching us. Once a friend who was dear to my heart failed to hide her critical eyes towards my arms-wide-open worship of the Savior. It embarrassed her, and her husband too. It drew too much attention.

Only took a few Sundays until the seats beside us were no longer filled by them. It was a grievous thing to my heart, but then, so like God, those seats were filled by souls who wanted to know more about this One we loved so deeply. They wanted more of Him, they needed more of Him. And the criticism of one was replaced as the goodness of the Cross came near for another. Too many of us grownups are too careful when we let love flow through us. Oh but not a child...

Sparks grow into flames as air passes over them. A spark never grows larger, if air doesn't rush over it. Blacksmiths can only forge metal on super heated flames. The horseshoe will never take good shape, the blade will never hold a good edge, and the temper will not set in the metal, unless the fire heats them deeply and the hammer lays them well. Air in lungs used sparingly lends no strength to whatever comes from them. Just as flames unfed by air will never give strength to the fire's forging ability.

My great grandfather was the town Blacksmith many by-gone years ago in the county where I grew up. His daily work involved fire and metal, air and water. I'm told he was a gregarious man who loved life, loved the Lord, and loved to work. He knew the importance of billows filled with air pressing strength into flames. From my Daddy's stories of him, it's most likely he also knew the importance of lungs filled deeply with that same strengthening airflow when lifting up his voice to the One who gave him both lung and air. It's just a strong guess, but it's safe to say those sitting near Pastor Porter on Sunday mornings knew how much he loved his Lord when he opened his mouth. In my mind I can imagine those walking past his blacksmith shop might have heard it through the week as well. Air from the billows heating the fire for the metal; air from his lungs pressing out worship while he hammered the metal into submission. I don't know this is true, but I'm allowed to indulge in the hope of it.

It's an odd sort of thing to ponder when singing to the Lord. Who thinks of billows in the long-lost days of Blacksmith shops when they're filling their lungs for another pressing out of love?

The little girl does. The one encouraged to sing it loud by the Sunday School teacher who smiled at the strength of the love flowing in the tiny block wall room in the basement of the little country church. And that little girl grew into a woman who navigated past the awkward teenage years of wondering who she was and why worship meant so much. She grew into a woman who came to realize worship is for the One being worshiped; worship is for Him alone. That woman knew the One she worshiped would carry her children from birth to death and hold them in all the hills and valleys in between their beginning and end. She knew the One to whom she let the air flow strong from her lungs and plink words of praise off her vibrating soul, was the Savior, the same One who had given all, so she could have all.

All that was worth having. All that mattered. She was the trembling lady who knew her need, and found her peace when she closed her eyes and let the air flow strong against the soul-sparks the world had tried to douse again. And the rush of worship-air rose up to the air-Maker, and the flames were fanned and strengthened for another surge of life's forging.

What my much-loved-friend was missing was the simple, solid fact, worship is for Him. How it sounds, how it looks, what it says, how sincerely it's given… it's all only for Him. To pause long enough to even consider the others who are present, is allowing something else to be worshiped in His place. What? Really? Yes. It's a soul-serious-thing.

When we think of what others might think, and we hold the free-flow of love back, then we are worshiping the opinion of others more than the One who is jealous for our praise. Or could it be that we are simply thinking more about ourselves? *But how will it make me look? Will I sound good?* Dear ones, remember, the One who hung on a cross after having the flesh peeled off him, never paused in those painful moments to consider how He looked or sounded.

He was too busy thinking of us.
What others thought of Him did not matter.

We get tricked into thinking it matters what we look like. What others will think, what others might whisper about us behind our backs. And it's a lie. What others think is only reflective of their soul. What others say are words heard most loudly by the One who loves us. And HE will defend us if we need to be defended. But what our Savior thinks, what our Savior says, has the ring of eternity to it.

The faithful Sunday School teacher with her 60's stylish attire and her cat-eye fashionable glasses, led the little warriors in tiny wooden chairs as they sang a tune first sung by slaves in fields crying out to be remembered by the Lord. The song was easy to remember, the words flowed just right:

"Do Lord, oh do Lord, oh do remember me,
Do Lord, oh do Lord, oh do remember me,
Do Lord, oh do Lord, oh do remember me,
Look a way, beyond, the blue."

It rolled into verses like:

"I've got a home in Glory land that outshines the sun...
I took Jesus as my Savior you take Him too...
Mine eyes have seen the glory of the coming of the Lord..".

If you knew the song as a child, and if you paused a bit to read over the lyrics above, I bet your foot is at least wanting to tap along to it again.

It's been years since the old song has curled through my mind. But then last week, in a bathroom stall in Nairobi, someone began humming it nearby. I was sick. Had run to the bathroom, and thanked God during the sprint that there was a bathroom to run to. Forgive my transparency, but it's shared with good reason. You see it's when we are lowest that we hear best. When we're down we can see better. When we're sick, we feel our need and when we're sick on a toilet, we can't be distracted by other things (hopefully we're in there alone).

I'd been sick for a few days, off and on. It wasn't anything serious, but I was not well. I was alone. Hurting. And so, I began to pray. Imagine the One I worship is also the One who will stay with meeven when I'mconfined to a restroom stall. He truly does not care how things look... He does not worry over what others might say. As I prayed, time passed by, and I began to wonder if I was ever going to be able to leave the unwanted seat I had been assigned. Then the humming started. Not from me, from someone nearby.

Ever so faintly, almost distant in its sound. My mind began clicking trying to find the familiar tune from the files of my childhood. Slowly the words formed. Some sounded wrong, I struggled to correct them.

"...look a way, beyond, the moon... no... it's not moon...
...look a way, beyond, the sun... no.. ah yes, it's the blue... look a way,
beyond the blue...
...do Lord, oh do Lord, ...remember me..."

The quiet lady, whose job is to tend the bathroom, was humming in the gentlest of ways. A song from my childhood, in a toilet on the other side of the world. My stomach slowly gave up its struggle, my head focused on the tune. She never uttered a word, she hummed as my mind sang along with her.

Day after day, she sits in the restroom, cleaning up messes left by others. No windows, no fresh air, just white tile floors to clean and toilet rolls to fill. But as she did her work, she hummed. What a humble position she has in this world. But, she doesn't seem to care what people think of her. She seemed thankful to have a job; she can feed her children. What others think just doesn't measure up to that.

This grown up little girl was taken back to the days of shiny black shoes and frilly socks, when momma and daddy were just down the hall and sister and brother were polished up and sitting smart in their Sunday best too. Where everyone knew her and had cared when she knelt down on her skinny knees, struggling to believe, that the good One would remember her, that the kind One would want her.

And now she was thankful a second time for the tissue paper, this time it was was needed for her tears. For they flowed sweetly over the way the One who remembers us always, came flooding in again. His Robes brushed by, even in a bathroom stall. You see, His girl was there, and so He would be as well.

The song was originally sung by suffering slaves at work in the field. (Oh Father, how cruel this world can be.) Then it came to children in pretty country churches in settings fit to be painted. Now it's hummed by a dear, silent soul working in a tucked away public toilet.

And You, Father, use it again to remind me that... You remember me. You remember us in the fields, when fresh lashes glimmered wet blood. You remember us in classrooms, where You were first introducing your-self to little ones. You remember us in the places no one notices, where no one wants to stay for long. You remember us when we're sick, and tired, and weak.

We are smaller than the tiniest fleck in the vastness of the worlds You have made. But still, You remember us.

So God, I'll remember You when I'min the field working. No blood glim-mers on my back, but may it always sparkle in my soul.

I'll remember You when I'min the classroom of this life, still getting to know You and Your ways. I'll remember You in the places I find myself, where no one else is near, no one would want to be. I'll remember You when I'mbeside the sick ones, the tired ones, the weak ones... I'll remember You to them.

You're the only thing I have that's worth remembering to them. You're the wonderful One I have, they need to know you remember them.

Gathering myself together, I emerged from the bathroom stall. No one was there, but I could hear the humming from the hallway outside. With hands washed and gratitude spoken in the mirror, as my reflection and me thanked the One who met us in this unpleasant place, my footsteps went straight to her. She smiled, looked down, and waited for me to pass.

"Were you just humming a song?"
"M-hmm, I was."
"What is the song called?"
So shyly, not sure of herself at all,
"It was Do Lord", do you know it?"
"Oh yes, I think I do, does it go like this..."
and I began to sing. Softly at first.

Her face lit up and quietly she sang as well. Then I felt the billows blowing inside. My great-grandfather blacksmith would have smiled I'msure, but more importantly, I could sense the nearness of white robes. So I sang a bit more loudly. Her smile grew as did her volume. And by the time we reached the end, we were singing like

Sunday School girls in frilly white socks, letting the flow of life echo off the cinder block walls around us.

Our names, our jobs, our color, our pains… they didn't matter. The One who remembers us both, was the only thing on both our minds. And we knew, He does remember us. Perhaps that's what matters most. When others see us, when others talk about us, when others remember us, may they be stuck with nothing more to say than, "they love that Lord of theirs."

Do Lord

I've got a home in glo-ry land that out-shines the sun,

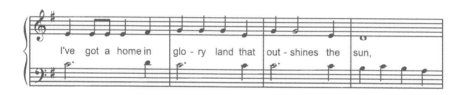

I've got a home in glo-ry land that out-shines the sun,

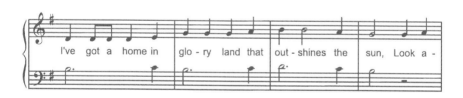

I've got a home in glo-ry land that out-shines the sun, Look a-

way be-yond the blue.

Do Lord, oh, do, Lord, oh, do re-mem-ber me,

Do Lord, oh, do Lord, oh, do re-mem-ber me.

Do Lord, oh do Lord, oh, do re-mem-ber me, Look a-

way be-yond the blue.

Written by Julia Ward Howe
also known for Battle Hymn of the Republic

FOUR

she dances

"A time to weep, and a time to laugh; a time to mourn, and a time to dance…" Ecclesiastes 3:4

While little Grace was still in her mother's womb, Jesus moved in beside her, into her mother's soul. Just as if He wanted to be sure she felt Him near.

Abandoned by her earthly father, her mother wept over how she would ever be able to feed four little mouths on her own. Life for a single mother in Africa is like paddling upriver e-v-e-r-y-day. There's the stigma of society that silently taunts "why do your children not have a father?" There's the struggle of putting a roof over their heads and food in their ever aching stomachs. Never-mind that the mother has remained faithful and had no power to hold the father to the place he should have stayed. So many things ache here. Mosquitos bring malaria. Bad water brings typhoid. Even the dirt here holds hidden parasites and jumping jiggers. But on that dirt dances a little girl who has mesmerized this writer with her worship.

Grace. She sparkles in an unassuming, silent way. She looks no different than all the others around her. Just one in a million of close shaved heads bouncing down a dirt road. But she is — different.

Her mother, Eve, shared with me once that she wondered at why God would choose to place one like Grace under her care. "What do you mean, Eve?" I asked. "It's just that Grace teaches me. She has no idea all I learn from her." And Eve began to share the holy-beauty of this little snaggle-toothed treasure. She said…

"When Grace talks to God she holds nothing back. She wails and cries knowing she is in a crowd of many, but calling out to have God's eyes come upon her alone. She neither notices nor ponders what another might think, for she is most interested in calling on the One who made her. She knows He loves her, hears her, cares for her. She knows. Not because she's been told it is so, but because she… well, she just knows it to be true."

Once while at their church and when Grace was just old enough to go to school, she asked her mother why her friends were beginning school the next day, but she was not. With gentle words, Eve explained, "Grace, I have no money to send you to school. But when

God gives us the money, you will go to school." Grace smiled. Looking down she walked slowly away, crossing the church to the far
distant corner where no one was sitting. It was not a Sunday, so few
were there. But Eve and her children often went to the church
during the week. They sometimes even slept there. When life is hard
at home, church becomes a refuge. Eve sat with a friend who had
taught her much as a young Christian mother, little Grace sought
the solitude of the corner.

Minutes later, cries were heard coming from Grace's corner. Eve
froze and strained to hear what was wrong. Faintly at first, but then
growing in strength, little Grace's words came, "God, I cry on you!
Really, God, I cry on you for help. You see, you know, you know what
is needed. You know my mother needs money to send me to school.
You know my brother needs to go with me. You know.. God... God...
oh God... you are the One to take care of us. My mother will send us
to school if you send her the money. But God, you must make a
way... I cry on you God."

"Nakulilia Mungu wangu"
swahili for "I cry on you my God"

All this gushed out in high pitched wails. Not in subtle, soft, polite,
proper whispers. No this little one was "calling" to God and crying
on Him. Eve began to move to stop Grace from disturbing the
others. Eve was concerned with the volume of her daughter's
words, she didn't want her child distracting others from their

grown-up-things. And Eve was herself, just learning the ways of God.

As she began to move towards Grace, the lady beside stayed her with these words, "Eve, we grown-ups need to learn from your Grace, she is wiser than we. You told her what was needed, she is asking. We sit and talk about our problems, she takes them straight to the One who can do something about them. She cares little for how she looks, she wants to see God. Grace is right. She is talking to God, and now we pray and ask, 'God will you please hear the prayer of little Grace.'"

The wailing prayers rolled into asking forgiveness for the wrongs of anyone in her house. Asking for God's help to show them all the way He wants them to live. "Help us Lord, forgive us, show us, forgive us..." The cries were high pitched and melodic. The kind that hold air still. After about 20 minutes of this (yes, twenty minutes of prayer from a 6 year old wee-warrior), Grace got up, wiped off her clothes, and walked home. That night there came a call on Eve's phone.

A neighbor was asking for Grace and Peter to be up early in the morning, prepared to go with her to school. Eve asked, "How can you take them to school, for I have not school fees to send with them?" The neighbor said, "Never you mind, just have them ready early." Then early in the morning Eve went to the church to pray as usual. As the sun rose, Eve returned home and awakened the children with instructions to get dressed and be ready for the neighbor's arrival. She spoke not of what the neighbor had said, the children were just to go with her. Eve held it in her heart, had God heard Grace's prayers?

Hours passed until evening, and finally Grace and Peter returned, with a full year's school fees paid and sporting new school uniforms. And Grace... well she danced and danced twirling herself about and moving every inch of her tiny frame, shouting in a sing-song way, "God you love me, really you love me. You have taken me to school and given what I asked. Oh God I thank you, God I thank you, really, God it is YOU who has done this. God surely you love me…"

Eve was learning from her six year old prayer-child. God had moved the heart of a missionary just the day before when Grace was praying. The missionary gave funds to cover school fees for twenty children and had asked the neighbor to find the best candidates. By nightfall, eighteen children had been found, but two were still needed. As the neighbor had prayed for two more children, Grace and Peter had come to her mind.

"Nakulilia Mungu wangu."
Translation: God, I cry on you! Really, God, I cry on you for help.

Tiny Grace has four pairs of shoes in this world. School shoes, church shoes, rain-boots, and rubber shoes. She dances in those shoes. How many pairs of shoes do I have? How many of them have danced for joy over the goodness of God? Oh God… I am learning.

This year the anonymous missionary was no longer able to pay for the children's school fees. But, another has done so and has paid all that is needed for the next 2 years. A little girl's prayers in the corner of a church moved Heaven. And perhaps the Father loves to see His little Grace dance!

One night at dinner time Grace sat back in her seat and said, "We always have vegetables, but never any meat. Mom, I want cow-meat to eat. Can we have some cow-meat?" Eve explained that cow-meat was costly and they were blessed to have vegetables. Grace threw back her tiny head and with a perfectly wonderful high-pitched tone said, "Lord, we thank you for the vegetables, they are good and we are glad for them. But would you please send us some cow-meat to eat? It would be so good to eat." Finishing her food she settled in to sleep. Eve smiled.

The next day Eve came to work and no sooner had she arrived but I called her into the kitchen and said, "Eve, yesterday I bought two packets of meat at the market. It is good beef, but I cooked one last night and it is just too tough for us. Would you be willing to take this one home with you and cook it long so it will be tender with your vegetables tonight?" Eve looked at me with a most curious look, but replied with a quiet, "Yes mom," as she often calls me, "I will cook it tonight." I was concerned that my gift of 'tough' meat might have offended. So I purposed in my heart to be more careful the next time.

The following day Eve shared with me how God had worked through Grace's prayers and how I, completely unaware of Grace's request to God, had handed her a packet of cow-meat the very next morning. Eve's curious look had only been an expression of shock at God's quick provision after Grace's prayer just the night before. Most beautiful was Eve's telling of how Grace had danced and danced and danced... when Eve had arrived home the evening before with a packet of cow-meat for their dinner. She danced and twirled and thanked God loudly singing, "God you love me, really you love me!"

And I'm learning.

How long has it been since I danced for joy over the goodness of God? David danced. David even danced naked... (that's not happening!) But he danced for joy.

"Let them praise his name in the dance..." Psalm 149:3

Have I held myself too carefully? Do I worry too much over what "they" might think? Is it the eyes around me or the eyes above me that matter most? In my inner most being, I know God loves for little Grace to dance.

I close my eyes and worship Abba as the music plays

and praise spills from my lips...
I close my eyes and reach with my hands...
I feel His robes brush my fingers tips…
and I'mtwirling at His feet.
He's High and Holy and God-of-All.
I'm His little girl twirling
and dancing around his great mighty feet.
His white robes gently whisk round me,
no one sees me,
no one knows
One sees me
One knows.
I'm His tiny dancing daughter
He's my Holy-Daddy-God.
He covers me and loves me and I dance...
and dance... and dance.
I close my eyes and worship Abba...
and dance around His robes.

"…[Christians] believe that the living, dynamic activity of love has been going on in God for ever and has created everything else. And that, by the way, is perhaps the most important difference between Christianity and all other religions: that in Christianity God is not a static thing–not even a person–but a dynamic, pulsating activity, a life, almost a kind of drama. Almost, if you will not think me irrever-ent, Christianity is to be a kind of dance…

"And now, what does it all matter? It matters more than anything else in the world. The whole dance, or drama, or pattern of this three-Personal life is to be played out in each one of us: or (putting it the other way round) each one of us has got to enter that pattern, take his place in that dance. There is no other way to the happiness for which we were made."

– C.S. Lewis, *Mere Christianity*

she dances

FIVE

winter trees & dandelions

Growing old is suppose to be a beautiful thing. It's the result of having lived many years and still having something to give, to do, to share.

Good grief how this world has twisted our view of growing old. I'mslowly approaching almost 6 decades of living. I'mgetting "older". Period. But if i've chosen to live well and love much – older won't be the focus, outflow will be. Here's to sharing with you, what Abba has whispered to me about growing better (aka older).

It's not about getting older. It's about increased outflow. Sitting on our mountain porch in December under wintry, grey, stick-like trees, it came so clear. Those tall oak trees stood brave and bear around me. The picture of winter. As a child I always thought they looked naked and cold. Not now. As a grown woman joyfully living in the autumn of my life, I see them with better eyes. You see, those tall trees have lived long enough to reach high above every man-made thing around them.

They remember what it was to be a tree in the spring, with sap rising, leaves budding, bark stretching, and birds nesting. They remember what the heat of summer felt like on their wide green leaves. The rains washed them clean and the sun dried them well. They remember the sounds of children under their shady branches and treehouses built on their strong limbs.

Then came the shocking beauty of their autumn. When the leaves they had grown began to sparkle with colors most extraordinary. No longer were they like every other tree in a coat of green. Now they were unique in their own personal coat of color. And they found their color looked even better beside the other colors around them. Red is pretty alone, yes. But put it beside a bit of yellow and a splash of orange and all together they become astounding! Exactly how it should be with us people.

Fall leaves speak so loudly, if we'll listen. They say to us, "I've lived well, I've grown. I have memories. And now, I get to bless everyone who walks near me. I'mnot longing for spring, I'mcelebrating the colors of autumn. I've had lots of sunshine days and soaking rains and i've stored it up so I can give this blast of color. My leaves can not hold it all in, they burst with the joy of living. The richness of the colors only speaks out of all i've seen and learned." The autumn tree says to the autumn soul, "You have so much to give. Do it with color and joy and life. Bust out of the confines of youth. Share boldly of the richness that life has brought you."

Next will be the winter. And in the winter of our lives, our leaves will fade in color, and fly. For the first and only time our leaves will do something they've never ever been able to do before. They fly. It should be true for us as well. In our winter, we should be able to do a new thing, something we've never done before. We should ever be learning and growing and producing. When we stop, we are no longer actually living.

The wind will pluck leaves from our limbs and they will fly. It's beautiful really. The Windmaker takes what we can offer and carries it to wherever He wishes. And we, like that winter tree, are not left naked and cold, instead we are unashamed and eager as we hide nothing and hold everything high. Look at that winter tree. Nothing conceals its long, strong branches as they bravely hold every limb as high as possible, reaching upward always. They are the picture of bare-bold-worship! They are not focused on trying to look pretty. They care nothing about hiding themselves in the folds of many leaves. They know fully what they're made of and they are singularly focused on what is above them. Amazing inspiration drips from their grey branches.

When we enter our winter years, what will fly from us? What will the

Windmaker be able to carry from us to the world around us? There is a final flight scheduled for us. Will the Windmaker find us having given all, hiding nothing, and boldly showing our reach for Him?

The worldly way will twist this beautiful imagery and distract us from seeing it. The worldly way says we must try and stay young, look young; it says if we're not young then we're not valuable. It says use this cream to remove dark spots, and this cream to minimize aging, have this treatment to plump up tired lines, and this procedure to take ten years off your face. But oh that's not the Father's plan. Take care of ourselves? Yes! Do the best we can with what we have? Yes! But could we please be real about what's real, and not waste time or money on trying to be something we are not. On something we were never suppose to be.

The leafy tree reminds us to embrace the season we are in. Enjoy the new life of spring. Love the warmth of summer. Indulge in the copious colors of autumn. And then be brave in the bare-bold-worship of winter.

There are many ways nature whispers the secret joys of age to us. Can you think of others? Look at the mountains. Formed from upheavals of volcanic earth activity, their "spring" is steep with sharp ridges. Millions of years pass until the "winter" of their development finds them softened in steepness and covered in green. The beautiful Appalachian mountains are the picture of this. The soil has finally tempered and has become a fertile place for new life to grow.

The mountain's "winter" is its most life-giving season.

One more? How about the dainty dandelion flower. It's a fascinating little circle of sunshine yellow. Since i've just written a book entitled "Dandelion: A Warrior Beside Him", i've taken much time to ponder this little jewel. It teaches so much in its silent presence. It too has a four season life span; it all occurs in less than a month. Its spring season bursts with a bloom of yellow joy. In this season its stem is usually shorter, holding it closer to the ground. Then summer finds it closing itself up looking almost as if it has not bloomed at all.

In the autumn of its living the stem grows long, sometimes increasing by several inches. Imagine the work that is taking place in that little flower during its summer and autumn stages.

But then finally comes its winter, when the closed up bloom opens itself wide forming a full round ball of seeds prepared to fly. It fascinates me that the round puff-ball even looks a bit grey, like the grey hair of us in our winter.

Compare the grey puff ball to its much younger version, the yellow flower. While the flower is a beautiful blast of color, it does not yet have the ability to produce the hundreds of seeds the grey-haired puff ball is able to give. The grey puff ball would be woefully amiss if it struggled over its loss of youthful color; what a waste of focus that would be. For indeed, the yellow flower was destined to close itself up so that in the end the ultimate purpose of its existence could be fully known. It must die to its youth in order to produce what is needed. New-life coming from new seeds.

It's a breathtaking reminder, that the grey puff ball sits perfectly still until the wind touches it, grabbing hold of its ready seeds and carrying them at will to the places of its choice. If not the wind, then a bird will indulge in the meal it provides and even still then, it will be carried on wings to many other places. And sweet is the picture when a child eagerly plucks the round seed head and "helps" the wind do its job. However it comes about, the end result is the same. The seeds are carried. The dandelion in its winter is able to doing something new, something it's never done before. It releases all it has left to give and life is multiplied.

One dandelion flower obediently living out its seasons of life will produce well over 100 seeds. More than one hundred new blooms will come because the one lived as it should have. Can we people say as much? Does the tiny dandelion do its work of living-and-giving better than we soul carriers?

If you're young, may this sharing encourage you to live each season exactly as it should be.

Don't strain ahead trying to grow into another season before it's time to be there. And someday when you're old, don't pine away over the loss of your youth. Each season has a wonderfully important purpose. Perhaps the winter season is the one of most intense value; it is the one where multiplication should be exponential if you've lived your other seasons well. If we can know this in our youth, we can set ourselves up for a most beautiful winter.

If your older, may this sharing encourage you to embrace the wintry gift of multiplication. When there should be nothing hindering our exposed worship with a life raised high and nothing limiting the wind from carrying us. If we've lived well, loved much, and grown in good ways, we now have the chance to fly as the Windmaker carries us wherever He chooses.

Perhaps you'll multiply goodness in the generations after you as they live out what you showed them. Or maybe you'll multiply your love of God and Savior as you're legacy travels far. Maybe your life-work will extend to places and people you never knew and in ways you never imagined possible. It's the very essence of the words, *"...to Him who is able to do far more... abundantly beyond... all that we hope for or imagine, according to the power that works within us, to Him be the glory... to all generations forever and ever. Amen."* (Ephesians 3:20-21)

There is more to give. More to do. More to share. More...

Notice how we can see further in the forest when the winter trees stand brave and bare. If we will be brave, bare winter trees, perhaps those younger than us can grow stronger beside us. Isn't it the way of the great forests.

J. C. Penney said, "I may be losing my ability to see in my old age, but my vision is better than ever before."

SIX

with paper dolls in a cardboard box

With cut paper doll toys in a cardboard box filled with sand, we lay on the grass under blue skies, and he told me a story.

He's a boy in Kenya, a boy with a story. But on this day, he didn't tell me "his" story. Instead, he shared one he made up in his mind. A story of forgiveness, coming from one who has solid grounds to hold unforgiveness inside. Allan is his name. I asked if I could share his story with many. His soft smile and gentle nod is why I now humbly share it with you.

He said...

_____

"Once upon a time there was a man, a woman and a baby. They lived in a small house together. They had a garden but nothing was growing there. One day they found a large parcel. They were excited. They hoped something special would be in the package, but when they looked inside, nothing was there except for one tiny seed. The man and the woman thought perhaps it was a bean seed, so they planted it in their empty garden.

"Every day they cared for the seed. They watered it and watched over it carefully. Day after day the seed grew until finally it grew into a tree. They were not sure what kind of tree it was until one day an apple grew on the tree. The man picked the apple and took his knife to cut it in half so they could share it for dinner, but when he did so, they found gold coins inside the apple. Wow! They were so excited. Never had they ever had so many coins.

"The family put the coins in their pocket and went to town to buy food. Each day they picked another apple from the tree. Each day they went to town to buy more food. Soon they had plenty of food so they began to buy other things with the coins found inside the apples from the tree. They bought new furniture and clothes and many things for their house. Then the man decided to build a very big house so his family could live in a nicer place with many things. The apple tree kept growing coin filled apples so the family was soon able to move out of the small house and into the big house.

"When the man and the woman saw their neighbors on the roadway or passed by them in town, the man and the woman no longer greeted them. They were so busy buying things for themselves they seemed to have forgotten their neighbors. When the family had lived in the small house they had always welcomed their neighbors and given them kind greetings when they passed by. But not now.

"The family was so busy picking apples and buying new things with the coins inside, they forgot to continue caring for the apple tree. The tree became unhealthy and was not able to give so many apples as it had before. Then one day the mother said, 'We must remember to water our special tree or it will die.' And so they did.

"Soon the apple tree began growing apples again. The family was very excited. One morning, when the apples were nice and ready, the father picked one and cut it open with his knife. But no coins were found inside the apple, only dust was found where the coins had been. The family was very sad. What would they do?

"In time, the family decided to sell all their fine furniture so they could use the money to buy food for their stomachs. Then one day the father said, 'We must sell this big house we built so we can buy food. We will need to move back into the small house where we use to live.' The family was very sad and hungry.

"One day the family heard voices. They saw their neighbors coming down the path leading to the small house. They remembered how many times they had not greeted their neighbors and even ignored them when they saw them in town. They were sad.

"The neighbors knocked on the door of the small house. The man and woman opened the door. How surprised they were to see their neighbors arms filled with food and water! They welcomed the neighbors into their house and knew they would never forget this kindness.

"And the lesson to my story is this...
We must always forgive."

————————

White clouds were floating overhead. Birds sang loudly. Dogs barked in the distance. Wind slid silently through tree leaves above us. And in front of me... sat a tiny teacher.

We sat in silence after the story ended. He smiled a shy "did you like my story?" kind of smile. I smiled a "that was a wonderful story" kind of smile. And I wondered... did young Allan know he was preaching a sermon better than any pastor in any pulpit? This wounded child was teaching me, the one who was working to minister to him.

I'd learned the lesson of forgiveness before. I'd memorized the scriptures and even told the Bible stories to others. I'd spent a whole year of my life repeating the simple words *"be quick to forgive and generous with grace Donna, quick to forgive and generous with grace"* and worked diligently to live the words, not just say them.

But never had the reminder come in such a way as this; with little dark-skinned hands moving cut paper doll toys across white sand. Narrations spoken in soft, lyrically laid words rolling from such a tiny tongue.

We can read of it in Matthew 18: 21-35. It's straightforward. Forgive others when they have wronged you or the Father who loves most will allow the *torturers* to torment. We don't forgive because the offender deserves it... rarely could they ever deserve it. We forgive because we are told to do so by the Father, and we can trust that He truly knows what is best.

Is it any wonder my blood chilled through and through as I sat with this child, who had been rendered deeds that required much to be forgiven, and forgiveness flowed all round.

with paper dolls in a cardboard box

SEVEN

have courage, be kind

A Hispanic mother in America

Rushing into the restroom, not wanting to delay those who would be waiting for me, I rounded the corner giving myself the shortest time possible to get in and out. But only three seconds into my self-allotted one-minute-window, she looked at me and shifted me at my core. Church was over, we'd lingered longer than the others, talking with much-loved friends we hadn't seen in years. The halls had begun to echo with our voices, we were the last in the building.

But this little treasure was found silently working, cleaning, wiping away the sloppy splatters left on the sink counters in the women's toilet I'd just flown into. Me a flurry, her all peace.

I smiled in response to her, she'd smiled first with her eyes, then with her lips. Everything about her smiled, in such a "little-but-powerful" sort of way. It was a startling sort of kindness. Me a flurry, her all peace. Mine was a hurrying kind of living, not anxious or troubled, just moving fast to beat the clock, but her wall of gentleness drained the rush right out of me and I knew something truly good was in front of me. Without a word from either of us, I knew she was a much-loved-daughter of the One who had made her.

It doesn't happen often to me, not like that. But when it does, I've learned to get ready. Something sweeter than we people can come up with is about to be handed to me, if I'll just have eyes to see and ears to receive. It's a "Be still and know that I AM GOD" moment, and He can do it a-n-y-w-h-e-r-e He chooses.

Attending to the reason I'd entered the room, I listened to her soft hum as she cleaned.

Then washing my hands, I appreciated the spotless counter and shiny faucets she had just wiped clean. Another lady was cleaning toilets, and mopping out each stall. Taking my used paper towel to wipe away my splatters of water I turned to look at the young lady and thanked her for doing such a nice job. There were three of them in all, silent, busy, working. When I spoke to one, they all froze.

They were not use to being "seen".
They were there to clean, not to be seen.

But their work was almost done for the day, this public restroom was cleaner than most kitchens. As I thanked all three ladies for taking such good care of the restrooms in our church, they humbly received my words of affirmation. Two were older, the one was perhaps a daughter, I shared my name and asked for theirs. The little package of peace was named Isabella. Her mother stood beside her, Isabella's gentleness had been taught to her by her mother; the love between them was rich. My guess is that their pockets held little, but their hearts were wildly wealthy and I wondered if they knew how wonderfully different they were; how their riches were showing in ways that can't be bought or sold.

We talked. The hurry I had entered with was no more. Isabella's mother shared that her daughter always wanted to come to work with her to help on the days she did not have school, "You see, it is a way we can be together even though I need to work" (make NO mistake here, this daughter was blessed to help her mother, no one was making her work). So... this daughter and mother were together, cleaning up messes left by others... thankful for a job... thankful for time together... serving others.

An uncontrollable gush of love pressed through me towards this girl and her mother. Words of affirmation were spoken, the mother's eyes sparkled, young Isabella leaned into her mother with a shy glow of appreciation over having been seen. A fifty foot yacht could not have stayed afloat under the weight of their love. And I knew, I'd been to church twice.

An African mother in Kenya

_____

The twins were celebrating nine years of living, it was their birthday. The cake was baked and decorated with colorful candles. The table was set with safari plates and napkins, there was even a silly pointy party hat waiting at each chair. It was the Sunday we were to fly home from Kenya, but first, we'd get to thank God for making "them", we'd make sure they felt our joy over the fact that they had been born. I'd asked their precious mother if we could give them a surprise party, she'd joyfully agreed, saying, "They've never had a birthday cake, oh how happy they will be!" At 11AM they came walking down our long, dusty drive, dressed in their sweet Sunday best. So excited to have been invited to "mum's and dad's", not knowing a party was bulging inside the walls of our small lake cottage. In truth, we were just as excited over their surprise party as we were over the fact that just nine hours later we'd be boarding a plane and headed home for a three month visit.

There's something beautiful beyond words when real joy shows on a child's face. Their joy was present because they were coming for a visit, all dressed up and feeling special just to know they were wanted and welcome and loved. Their joy was present even before they knew of the party we'd prepared for them.

The mother and children walked towards our cottage, laughing together. Enjoying each other, they are thankful for more things than many people ever pause to notice. This family lives in one room, all together. They love living with no walls between them. As they approached our porch, we swung the doors wide open shouting, "Happy Birthday!" The children froze. Then slowly, after sweetly removing their dusty shoes (no one asked them to, they do it as a show of respect), they walked towards the table in awe of the colorful party plates and napkins.

They didn't know what to do with the pointy hats, our son Peter helped them there. Soon party hats were on and party horns were blowing — oh the pure pleasure of watching them celebrate their own birth in a way they'd never imagined before.

They're birthday cake was a chocolate sheet cake — just like the one I'd baked for all our precious three kids for all their wonderful birthdays back on Mockingbird Road. Grace and Peter's birthday cake eagerly waiting for them, resting in the same-same pan I'd used to bake Mike, Maggie, and Peter's birthday cakes. If a metal pan could speak, well, that one's had a sweet life.

Presents were given: a tiny dollhouse for Grace, four toy cars for Peter. Candles were lit, we all sang together. Eve, their mother, was even more excited than her nine year old treasures as she watched her love towards them be multiplied before her eyes. She'd struggled intensely just to put food in their mouths for seven of those nine years. But when God moved us to Kenya, He gave her a job working in our home. Our obedience was about so much more than us. God put the puzzle pieces together that needed to be in place. Eve needed a job, we needed help, her children needed food and school and a safer place to live. And on this day we were celebrating together — the goodness of the Lord.

Their older sister Faith sat at the table as well. She's beautiful in ways unable to be captured by camera or words. Poised humility — that's her. It's as if she's a princess whose chosen to live with less rather than more. There's a Cinderella-ness to her, she's gentle and caring, seeking nothing for herself, yet you get the real sense of knowing she's always in her Father's eyes, held very close to His heart. No matter that her earthly father abandoned her... her REAL FATHER holds her dear.

When candles were blown out and cheers were finished, without a word from anyone, little Grace bows her small head and begins praying. She's serious about her Lord, we all feel like children beside the maturity of her soul.

She prays long... not quickly...

She has her first birthday cake e-v-e-r in front of her — but she won't be rushed, she must thank her Daddy-God. Oh the lessons little Grace could teach the world. Then there's cake on plates and juice in cups, presents are opened, and photos snapped. We've done it, we've celebrated how thankful we all are that GOD MADE Grace and Peter! But where we are thinking we're finished, Faith softly clears her throat and Grace and Peter smile.

Eve smiles like a proud mother, as Faith leads her sister and brother singing a song naming the books of the Bible... all of them... all-of-them... in order. We are stunned!! And then, they begin quoting scriptures, perfectly. They're not struggling, no, those Holy Words come rolling off their little nine year old tongues just as easily as chocolate cake just passed over them.

Faith has been teaching her little brother and sister all these things, not with a whip or stick in hand, but with the gentlest of hands and the kindest of ways in the single room where they live.

"Have courage, be kind", words from the latest Cinderella movie — never seen by beautiful Faith, but beautifully LIVED in her every waking moment. Faith loves Grace and Peter, they love her, and Eve covers them all with such a loyal mother's love. It's not just words I'mtyping. It's real. She's a mother alone filling stomachs with food and hearts with love and pouring Jesus into the souls she's been given charge over. It's all so captivatingly beautiful. It's another glimpse of church. There's no steeple overhead, but HE is present and pleased.

———————

In this world, there are beautiful ones. They are self-less and undemanding. They are busy working and sharing and helping. They are poised and ready to teach, but they won't force themselves on others. They don't think of themselves as wise or "able" or important or strong. They don't criticize or judge, they don't have time for that, they are too busy in the middle of being courageous and kind. The world won't like them...*oh Father*... the world most likely won't be kind to them…

Little Isabella might be ridiculed and looked down on by those who think they're important, those who criticize, those who judge.

Lovely Faith might be lustfully looked at by those who are strong in dark ways, those who take, those who are not kind.

But Lord, You adore them. They are priceless masterpieces formed in your hands. They live more wonderfully than the ones who are loud and in front.

You've given Isabella and Faith to women who are precious and rare. Women who work hard and love well and care nothing for drawing attention to themselves, for they have the pleasure of feeding the mouths you've given them to feed, and they do it with hands roughened by work and strengthened by You.

So Lord, thank you for sharing Isabella and Faith with me, with us. Thank you for the quiet, seen, gentle, strength You teach us by the way these courageous, kind ones live. You are the One who says the "first will be last and the last will be first" and I'm oh so thankful for Your ways.

Because I will be eagerly perched and ready to cheer these two beauties on when YOU move them from the positions of "last", this world holds them in, and they are placed at the front of the line of those who have found great favor in Your ever watchful eyes.

Lord, they are lovely. Please protect them fiercely... please place a wall around them that holds back those who would do evil against them. And Lord, please continue to multiply your goodness in them, so that those who think they belong in the front, those who would look down on those they think are behind/beneath/below them, would instead be overwhelmed and amazed at the beautiful ways You are found. Where kindness and goodness and gentleness and faithfulness live.

Have courage — be kind.
Love God — love others.

have courage, be kind

EIGHT

three perfectly timed words

Did she know God was flowing through her? How beautiful, a middle-school aged girl, who sees and speaks three perfectly timed words... "You are beautiful."

She laughed, riding on her giggling friend's back. They were full of joy; it overflowed. Walking across a field, these two gregarious girls and the woman with them met a short haired woman, walking alone, who was a bit bewildered, needing directions. She asked their mother for directions, trying to learn the best way to get to where she needed to go.

After receiving the needed help, the small group spoke cordialities of "thank you's" and "have a good day," and walked on. But in the last minute passing, the young teenager did something quite remarkable — something every grown-up could take a lesson in. She broke the "rules" of sociatal norms and knowingly or unknowingly did God-work. The girl looked directly at the short-haired woman, reached inside her and touched her soul as she said,

"You are beautiful."

The woman paused for a moment, stunned. The young girl had no idea what she had just done, she most likely still has no idea. But for certain, her words went deep. Simple words, spoken with sincerity, breathed *life* into the woman who had just two days earlier finished her final radiation treatment after an almost six month battle against an invisible enemy that had threatened to end her life.

On Feb. 2, which also happened to be the short haired lady's 53rd birthday, the voice on the phone had said the words none of us ever want to hear, "the test results show, it is cancer..." Life shifted on that day. The weeks and months that followed found her in many doctor's offices, learning what she needed to know, to do her part in fighting the battle. She learned all about which wig would work best when her hair fell out, what foods would work best when her body was depleted, which hospital, which doctor, which clinic, which procedure... She entered into a classroom she did not want to attend and was given the class syllabus for a course she did not want to take.

This beautiful short haired lady is a nurse. She cares for people. She's done so for almost 30 years. She can put an IV into the tiniest hand of a premature baby, she can smile at a sick, pain-filled person in such a way that the medicine becomes secondary to their relief. She would prefer caring for others, than to be cared for by others.

Beautiful was not a word she had indulged in much of late. Living had been her focus.

Her first chemo treatment put her in bed for a day. But within the week, she was back caring for others. They had no idea the lady taking care of them was fighting a battle herself, between life and death. Her hair gave way as expected.

We had lunch together that day, then drove to my house, met Maggie, and perched ourselves outside under the great wisteria "tree" to let her hair fall among the thousands of purple flower petals surrounding us. Beautiful was the imagery, just as God will bring purple blooms again so we would trust Him to restore her hair. He is the One who makes all things new.

The second chemo treatment brought her to her knees for an extended time. She needed the touch of her Father to quiet the lies of His enemy. Had He forgotten her? Was she being punished? Would He keep His promises to her? Heavy questions. No audible answers came as we prayed together on that carpet, but the Healer was present, and the sun seemed to rise...around 3pm that afternoon.

The third chemo treatment held no new surprises. The hard days were exhausting, but she quickly recovered. She put "Snook" in place (the name she laughingly gave to her wig), carefully applied makeup to help disguise the thinned brows and lashes, and pressed forward. She is a remarkable lady.

The fourth treatment was old news. It was the finale hit, it did its work, she persevered, with a firm grip of His robes. Then came the radiation. Exhausting. Draining. Six weeks of continuing the fight against a hidden enemy by laying still on a table and being shot with radiation. Her body withstood the physical battle, her mind endured the emotional roller coaster.

Last week, she sat at our table; a table filled with food, chairs filled with family, hearts filled with thankfulness. She is with us. What a gift it is to share air.

Only those closest to her would have known how unsure of herself she felt that next day. She wanted to look pretty for her husband, they would be outside all day long in the hot Alabama heat to cheer for her sweet nieces as they played ball. She wanted to be free of Snook, she felt keenly aware of the lovely ladies around her, with their stylish hair and fashionable attire. That sly, ugly enemy of our Lord, wanted to make her feel as though the battle she had just endured had left her drained and somehow lessened. He's such a hideous liar, he watches for the weak moments and pounces. Like a wild animal on a helpless lamb.

But wait... our Lord knows this. And He's not inattentive or unaware. Our Savior knows we are lambs and we need a Shepherd. King David too must have felt lamb-like and in need of a Shepherd when he wrote, "The Lord is my shepherd, I will not be in want. He makes me lie down in green pastures, he leads me beside quiet waters, he restores my soul. He guides me along the right paths for his name's sake. Even though I walk through the darkest valley, I will fear no evil, for you are with me; your rod and your staff, they comfort me.

"You prepare a table before me in the presence of my enemies. You anoint my head with oil; my cup overflows. Surely your goodness and love will follow me all the days of my life, and I will dwell in the house of the Lord forever." Psalm 23

Is it possible that when all the hair let loose from her head, that the anointing oil could cover more deeply? And can a cup overflow, even when nothing looks or even feels right in our world?
Yes, because of the Shepherd.

The young middle-school aged girl who looked at her could not have known the doubt that was pestering the lady. But the Shepherd knew.

He knew His lamb needed to sense His good pleasure over her, He knew His enemy was prowling near. So, He flowed His words through the twinkling eyes of a teenage girl. He opened her eyes to see the beauty of the lady in front of her. And she opened her mouth and spoke words of life, and truth, and goodness.

Three perfectly timed words, "you are beautiful..." And the short-haired lady, who is my dear sister, was deeply moved because she felt God's touch through another.

Did the young girl have any idea she was speaking for God and silencing the ugly enemy? Most likely she did not know... but I'mso thankful she let the overflow of her heart see my sister, and then have the courage to acknowledge to her, "you are beautiful!"

God's work. Overflow.

And the enemy lay defeated as the little, cared-for lamb skipped on across the green pasture.

NINE

changing my focus & thinking of you

Are we getters or givers?

Do we wake up to bless or be blessed?

What's sitting at our bottom line?

Are we going through the motions of just another day? Silently working to get, do, have, become what we think matters most. Is today and tomorrow about us and ours… or is it about Him and them?

Long ago a friend told me, "Donna, when you are struggling (over hurts of the heart) the best solution is to turn it outward. Turn your eyes and your heart to look in front of you and see someone else. Don't look in the mirror. Don't look inside yourself. Just fix the eyes of your heart on the someone God brings in front of you, and then do something about what He lets you see."

It might look like a plate of cookies or a note, it might be an invitation to dinner, it might be a text or a call. It might be a prayer. A real, heartfelt, changing-my-focus-and-thinking-of-you prayer. It might be that the simple act of praying for someone is the best thing you can do for them (and oddly enough for yourself too). It's one of those "double portion things", your giving-out gives a good splash back.

But it all revolves around what we choose to do with "self". Do we think more about ourselves and our wants than we do of the other person and theirs? Do we even pause to honestly assess this part of our lives?

Jesus said we should consider the interests of others, their needs, their pain. We should also care for ourselves, we are not told to ignore our own selves (Philippians 2:4). But the order is crucial. If we "look to our own interests" first, we are compelled to linger at that level. "I" is too powerful, it demands much and is rarely fully satisfied. The One who made us knows. We are selfish and self-centered by nature. So He asks us to consider others, *look to the interests of others*, care-for-others.

So do we?

In the mornings when we open our eyes, what are our first

thoughts? Do they go to others? Or do they begin with "I"? What I need to accomplish, what I want to get, where I need to go?

Or are our first thoughts "help them Lord, help me Lord"... remembering that He knows the plans HE has for us in the day ahead. He knows what opportunities will stand in front of us. He also knows what hindrances will come. And sometimes we are our own greatest hindrance.

Our insides are so bare in those sunrise moments. We haven't had time to cover them up yet. And if we don't choose well at the beginning, how can we imagine a good end?

Recently I asked someone, "Do you wake up to be a blessing or do you wake up looking to be blessed?" The question sat long in the air between us. Blessed by God, yes, but I wasn't talking about that. The old phrase, "What's in it for me", becomes the wake up revelry for the person whose self has become too important. *What are our waking thoughts?*

Self wakes up wanting more. Its appetite is insatiable.

The new lamp I bought yesterday would look better
with the drapes I've been wanting,

but now this old couch looks shabby,
so I'll need to look for a new one,
and then, oh yes, that rug would be perfect.

The new fishing pole needs a better tackle box,
and if I'mgoing to do this right, a new boat.

Taking better care of myself means a gym membership,
which requires new gym clothes,
and then who could bear to look at those spider veins on my legs,
so I might as well get those fixed,
while I'm at it I should just go ahead and get that tummy tucked.

(Ignoring the fact that the money spent on self-image alone could make a life-difference for those who will never need a tummy tuck because their stomachs stay empty day in and day out!)

After all, we work hard right? We've earned it. You only live once and someday we'll wonder why we didn't get it while the gettin' was good.

———————

Oh Lord, what are we thinking?! We forget that someday we will wonder about the choices we will make today. We will wonder...

What of the mother whose daughter is watching, silently, learning from what she sees more than what she's told. A dear friend recently shared her heartbreak after chauffeuring a group of young teen girls around for a weekend of church activities. The car fairly vibrated with giggles and chatter. One topic led to another until all were in the air. And my friend was grieved to hear the jibber-jabber over the recent release of a movie that twists and contorts intimacy. I don't even want to type the title here, but sadly most readers will know of the movie the girls were talking of.

They were curious, they had heard others talk about it. Their mothers had talked with friends about it, in ways that didn't turn the girls from it, but instead drew them towards the dark mystery. Mothers speaking openly of their own fantasized intrigue only spoon fed their daughters an invitation to darkness. Mothers, thinking of themselves and their dissatisfaction, but forgetting the beautiful young eyes watching them and listening to every word.

Mothers who have perhaps slept with a self-absorbed husband who cared more about himself than the one in his arms. Mothers, who have perhaps responded with their own self-absorbed desires, and would consider reading a book or watching a movie to spice up their bedroom moments (with their husband or…).

Mothers who have carelessly stirred their daughters curiosity to see something that is hell's best shot at destroying intimacy. It's in those moments, when listening ears are learning what will not serve them well in life. Someday we will realize the impact our choices had on those around us, on ourselves and on the work of Heaven.

'Cause yes, the work of Heaven or the work of hell, they are both watchful for moments to flow through us to those in front of us.

But we forget. Jesus said it clear, "Thy Kingdom come, they will be done. "The Kingdom of Heaven is to come here, to be with us now. I'mnot speaking of the eternity we are promised in Heaven (for those who believe). I'mspeaking of the work of Heaven now.

We are not actually wired to wake up thinking this way. If we were, it would be automatically accomplished in each of us everyday, and life would be sweeter to drink.

Instead, it is a choice. It's something we are given the chance to do. We can open our eyes and choose to think of others, love God, live well, bring laughter, and think with purpose on how to live today. It would make tomorrow more beautiful. The enemy of our Lord knows this full well. Even if we choose to ignore or overlook it. He doesn't. And his dark scheme is to distract us in every way possible.

One of his favorite tools to distract us is the "self" that we live with. If he can just keep us focused on ourselves, our wants, our "needs", our desires, our image, our happiness, our sorrow, our emotions, our hurts... well then, he's got us beaten before we even get out of bed in the morning. If we focus on self, Heaven won't be flowing through us that day.

But he knows we are clever enough to catch on to his dark plan eventually. In those moments, we wonder why our friends aren't coming around anymore, our kids don't linger once they're able to stand alone, the one we married finds other places they need to be, or the earthly beauties around us seem lost and unfocused. When something is said or read or sung that gives us pause, and we begin to wonder... *why do I feel so empty and alone?* It's then he will slide in the thoughts of "self" in another frame, "look at all you've done, you're a good person, you do this and this and this, you can't do 'that', don't feel badly, after all you can only do so much..." We are unaware of how self-absorbed we have become.

Erik Erikson speaks of the last stage of human development as being the time in life when we face either despair or ego-integrity. Ego-integrity means the acceptance of life at the approach of the winter of our lives. When we face the victories and the defeats and allow ourselves no excuses or explanations, we see the true value of what we have accomplished and the grave loss of what we have not.

Those last days, those sunset years, we no longer have the energy or time to blame others or give justification for what we did or did not do. Because in those last days, we know the truth of what we lived for. Those who have lived with integrity and in life-giving ways, they can turn to face impending death and smile. But those who have lived for "self", face despair. They've wasted the thousands of sunrises and overlooked the beautiful sunsets. They wrestled with life to get their way, but in the end, it wasn't enough and it only has left a shadow of failure. The money, the house, the clothes, the status... none of it matters when those last breathing moments come.

But what we've done for others... how we've loved others, why we've loved others, when and where and how often we've loved others... those are the moments that will make us smile as we breathe our last earth-air. If our outflow to others is rich from the Heaven-flow in us, then God waters our garden so that others can have flowers aplenty on their tables (and maybe food too).

Are we getters or givers?
Do we wake up to bless or be blessed?
What's sitting at our bottom line?
Today, we get to choose. Tomorrow, it will matter.

TEN

finding a new way in an old wave

PART 1 It happens, things get broken

She shared words that were hard in coming. Words that told a story she wished had never been written. I said in the softest flow of air, "You can't stop what's happened, but you can choose a different ending than the one you're in now."

No vase would choose to be shattered. No heart asks to be broken. And when things break, the world would say it has been ruined. It is useless, it is finished. But the world is wrong... again.

Because the One who is above all things looks at that same broken-ness in a wiser way, with a keener eye. He says He can bring beauty from a pile of ashes. He can bring streams of water in the desert. He can take what seems ruined and make it new.

It's the way of brokenness.

Few will invite it to come. Most refuse its approach. Usually we have no choice. So rather than allow it to complete its work in us, we fight it, deny it, medicate it, or sometimes just run from it,

When we've known the hammer blows of personal brokenness, and lived to see the smoothing out of something rough in us, then we begin to understand its importance. But until we've known its effectual work, we struggle to sit still in its unsettling presence.

It's one of the huge differences between living in a first world place and a third world place. The contrast is stark. In a third world environment, there are few ways to escape the "thing" that is working to break you. You have no option, you can't simply go to another place and begin doing a different thing. Need and hunger hold you still. But in a first world place there are options, ways to get away from the thing that is pressing down. You can move, change jobs, find a new relationship, pull out the card and buy a new life.

But what if you're a child and the brokenness is coming to your parent, who is not covering you, and their brokenness rolls into your little world. You can't escape it. In a third world country like Kenya, this is exactly how too many street children come about. They run from the breakage, they eat from the dumpster, and a different broken begins to breathe. Or what if the breaking comes in the form of a disease. Even in a first world place, there's no way to hide from its impact. It's just that brokenness is a universal thing. It comes in every corner, and to everyone. Yet when it comes to us, when it's painfully personal and standing on our doorstep, we can feel so alone. Alone is not good. We were not created for aloneness.

She knew that something was gravely wrong. Tears came as her tongue stuck to the roof of her mouth. Our toes dug into the sand, we watched families playing in the waves, the sun began to set. She'd endured life, and worked to overcome much pain, but her past was haunting her present and fear was crashing in again.

Grave – it's the right word for it.

She could smell the pungent stench of death, her eyes could only see the struggle around her. And her strength, all of it, was being consumed (and wasted) on trying to maintain, survive, endure, and find a way to defeat the problems before her. And they weren't just her problems anymore. They were the problems being lived out in the lives of her children now. Their hurts carried a faint echo of her own, though they knew nothing of her story. She had held it silent for all her 60 decades. It looked exactly as though the other person in this painful "Life-Play", was the cause of the stench. It was their sin, their fault, their wrongdoings that caused the problems. And to a very large degree, this was oh-so-true!

If they would just change.... or perhaps if they had just disap-peared… *Could they just go away please? Then this suffocating dust could settle and the sun might shine again and life could get back on course... perhaps happiness could then come.*

But as surely as that solution seems so right, it would only be a tem-poral reprieve. For that would be the outward way of *relief* not the inward way of *healing.*

When the struggle inside us collides with the hammering-tool outside us (the situation, the person, the sickness, the "problem"), our eyes become fixed on IT, the problem. We put our focus on IT. We laser in on IT. And all our mind can think on is "if this thing was changed, I could find peace". IT is the problem. Right? But what of the Holy Words that say, "In this world you will have trouble. But do not be afraid. For I have overcome the world." (John 16:33) Doesn't that mean that in this old world, there are going to be so many "its"? Struggles will abound. Problems are "normal". Oh but I cringe even typing those words. It's a hard reality, not a sparkly, feel good truth. It's raw. Troubles come, then they go… then others come. The woe-is-me-soul would want to throw in the towel and give up on life. But not the Jesus-in-me-soul.

Have you ever walked on the ocean's shore, sand under you, sun above you, and waves steadily pounding beside you? There's a rhythm to the steadiness of it all; on most days it comforts us in some inner way. Then the sun gets too hot and we long for the coolness of the water. We inch our way in, toes first.

As she spoke, the waves beside us seemed to speak as well, "keep going, we're not shocked by anything you might say". They invited her every word, they were not afraid. Waves know what to do with the dirt of life. The cool waters felt good to our feet, so we kept moving forward. As we made progress into the waters, we came to that place where the waves crest. Where they peak and then fold, tumbling down in a ribbon of white rush. That's the line where, if the wave has any size, we might get knocked down. When we walk to the line of the rolling waves, we either choose to let it knock us over OR we choose to lean into it. The former means the wave is unbroken and it will carry us where it wants to. That's usually a whirl of confusion in foaming, sandy waters. But the latter means the wave line is broken and we find ourselves still standing on the other side of impact. Either way, something gets broken. Either the wave line is breeched or we are.

If you've ever found yourself coming against a big wave in the ocean, you know this: you have to brace yourself, even crouch down, bend your knees and lean forward to be able to endure the impact. For me, those big waves require that I... bend my knees. I've never once conquered a wave with straight, board-like legs. Try as you might, you can't do it. It's the bending of my knees that gives me balance.

It's the bending of our knees that gives us balance.

PART 2 Facing The Waves Wisely

In this sharing, the waves represent the "in this world you will have trouble" part of that verse. Unbent knees, stiffness, will not serve us well when facing those waves. Bent knees, a lowering of ourselves, better allows us to withstand the impact, and find ourselves in a new place. We're not bending our knees to give in to the trouble, no, we're bending our knees to balance ourselves against its impact. Have you ever noticed how calm the water is just beyond the wave line? Calm at least until the next wave comes.

Too often we might think of the wave line as the place where we should become strong, rigid, firm. We think if we get tough, we can beat the wave. But it's not our strength that will get us on the other side of the impact. More Holy Words speak directly to this thought of rigid strength winning. "Not by power, not by might, but by my Spirit say the Lord." (Zechariah 4:6) The way of the world says, get stronger, meaner, tougher. Fight fire with fire! If they hurt you, you hurt them more. But that world-way doesn't fit with the Abba-way. Jesus showed us clearly, His greatest show of strength came on that cross. He stayed there during the breaking. Then His greatest show of power came at the mouth of that tomb.

Our willingness to face the "wave" wisely *(in this world you will have trouble)*, to "bend our knees" *(do not be afraid)*, and choose to focus on the calmer waters beyond *(for I have overcome the world)*, this will carry us through.

It's not the removal of the wave that is needed. The waves are there, they will always be there, they will not be removed… until Heaven. If it's not this person, it will be another person. If it's not this challenge, it will be another like it. If it's not this unkind situation, it will be another. The waves are always there. And if we can r-e-a-l-l-y understand this at a soul-deep-level, we'll find a storehouse of grace and mercy for those around us who are being tossed about in waves of brokenness.

It's not the removal of the waves that will finally bring us happiness or peace or calm. It's our willingness to face them, and allow our bended knees to break the impact that will bring us to new places in life. What happens to the wave? If you've ever bent your knees, lowered yourself, closed your eyes, held your breath, and leaned forward into a wave, you find that you can endure it. The whirl of its waters will pass by. Then the wave continues on to where it was going. But it has not carried you with it. It might even lift your feet off the ocean floor briefly, but if we hold our position, it can not carry us with it. Therefore, our stance does not change the wave. We can not change the waves. We can not complain about them enough, argue with them enough, fight back against them enough, or in any way alter them. We have no control over the waves.

What we can do, what we do have a control over, is how we choose to face it. It is our only chance at altering the outcome. It can either throw us backwards onto the shore and crash its waters all over us, or we can choose to bend our knees, lower our center, and lean into it. The waves of life, they might intimidate us with their size, they might hit hard when they come, but oh… with *bent knees* and a *lowering of self*, they will not push us backwards into old places.

So this means that I can't face the waves without bending my knees and lowering my center of gravity. Those two things must be in place. Two things that will allow a breakthrough, but two things that will also allow a "breaking" in me. It's a very different kind of "breaking". Not the brokenness that comes from the hand of another; it's rather a brokenness that comes IN the hands of the FATHER.

Bending my knees is that visual reference to praying. Bending myself, no stiffness of leg or heart or mind or emotion. (This is a hard thing to do if we're stuck in the "i must defeat it" mode.) Bending my everything to HIM, not to it or them. It means I must grab hold of His robes, look for His way, choose His hand on my heart. No more shaking my fist at the wave. Instead choosing His way in the wave. Trusting that He really is good and He truly can carry me through the impact(s) of this life and in so doing, He will be washing me with each wave. He will be washing something from me that needed to go, something I hadn't even realized was stuck to me. And when I will allow the truth to really come through, I'll realize the stench I thought was on another, was actually also on me. Only Abba can wash that stench away with His blood. It's the work of our Savior to master the waves, as we bend our knees to Him.

For just a few lines, I'll share of one wave that repeatedly crashed into my world and left me covered in scratchy sand. For all my life I've been eager for friendship. Even as a little girl, having friends around me, good friends, meant all was right with my world. Somehow I was wired to enjoy friendship. But throughout my life there have been sad stories of friendships gone wrong. Not all my friendships, thank God, for there are many who have journeyed closely with me for all my days. What a gift. But still there have been several key friends who I treasured so much, who I walked closely beside, but then suddenly they stepped away. Disappearing, sometimes even hurting me in the process. Never once did any of those "friends" come to tell me what I'd done to cause their rejection. Even if I went to her, there would be no reason given. Just an abandonment of the friendship, and I'd be leveled by the wave.

Some people, of different temperaments than mine, don't care so much when a friend moves on. But it's been a wave that has pounded me more than once in my life. The last time this hard wave came, I lifted myself up to Jesus and said, "Please help me, I need help here, this hurts too much." I bent my knees to Him, lowered my center (myself and how I felt), and asked Him to wash me, wash off of me what needed to go to be healed from the inside out. And He showed me something IN ME that He wanted to "clean up" (change). The wave can wash us. It might not touch the one who has hurt us, but it can wash us in good ways.

What was it in me that needed to go? What needed to be washed away?

He was jealous for my focus. He did not want me to be so focused on that friend; what they thought, if they cared, if they responded or walked away. He did not want their actions towards me to matter nearly as much as I was allowing it to matter. He wanted me to lean in to HIM, and not lament over them. Period. It was that simple. And in the bending of my knees in the wave, Jesus said, "Pray for them, give them to me, I'll take care of them, YOU FOCUS ON ME, I will never leave you."

John 21:22 came alive for me, "If I want him to remain alive until I return, what is that to you? As for you, you follow me." Paraphrased and personal for me it became, "If I want them to… go another way… what's that to you donna? As for you, my instruction is clear: you follow me."

This is a small thing in life, right? For some it is. For others it can be debilitating. For me it was bigger than it should have been. I'm letting you see the bottom side of my scrapings as I dare share it here. The point is waves come in different sizes and with different strengths. Small or big, if a wave has the strength to knock us down, then it needs to be handled carefully, faced wisely, and dealt with completely. It needs to be approached and measured and honestly laid before the One who will use it for good in our lives. We need only to hold His hand at the wave-line. Bent knees. A lowering of me. Little or big, if something wounds, learn from the wave you leaned into before! Next time you find yourself near those strong ocean waves, do yourself a favor and experience a visual of this.

Don't laugh at me here, resist the urge to roll your eyes (cause you're gonna want to).

Find a spot on the beach all to yourself. This is not a spectator "sport". Carry a bottle of ketchup with you, the cheaper the better. Stand at the shoreline and pour that ketchup all over your arms and legs. You'll feel goofy for sure, but only for a second or two. Then walk your sauce-covered-self out into the water up to the wave-line. Bend your knees and lower your center of gravity. Brace yourself for the waves, don't let them break you, instead you break their line. Stay there for wave, after wave, after wave. With each wave you'll find you get more accustomed to the stance you need to have, how low you need to go, how much you need to bend your knees. You'll get tired, yes. But you'll get wiser in the ebb and flow of those waves. Let 10, 12, 15 waves come and go, then turn and walk back to the shore. Look at your arms and legs. Is there any red ketchup left? There won't be. What was on you will have been washed from you as you focused on bending your knees and lower-ing yourself. Is it a silly visual or a solid picture of truth? (maybe both)

Now, be honest with yourself and with the One who already knows the answer to every question. What's the cheap ketchup mess in your life? What is stuck to you that needs to go? Because if it gets to stay, it will bring a world-brokenness inside you. How many times have you felt its stickiness in your life? Be honest with God about it, right now, and ask Him to help you as you bend your knees, praying over it again and again. Then lower yourself before Him, so He can increase in you. Ask Him to show you the new way you need to allow a cleansing brokenness (from Him) to wash the sticky mess away. It won't happen in a day, or even a week. For me it almost always takes a steadiness in many waves to finally walk back to the shoreline and feel "clean of it". But begin today dear one. Begin today.

PART 3 Wash me Lord, use those waves to wash me.
Broken for GOOD.

Lowering yourself, lowering your "center" so the wave doesn't catch you off balance and throw you backwards is the picture of John 3:30 "I must decrease and He must increase." Oh how we struggle in the living out of those 7 little words. For we think we must increase, we must get stronger, we must press our point or win the fight or prove them wrong or take our revenge in order to beat "the wave". But this, dear one, is the lie of the evil one.

We can not beat the waves with stiff, strong, unbent legs.
We can not stop them from coming, we can not alter them.

But if we will decrease and choose to increase Him, we find there is a bedrock strength under us in the wave. It is He who then causes the wave to wash us as it passes by, and we find ourselves in a strange new place of still waters. Watchman Nee writes so beautifully of this lowering of our center. His words call it a choosing of brokenness, an allowance of God's dealings. His book "The Release of the Spirit" has filled my plate of late, and opened my eyes to much.

Brokenness.

Brokenness is something to be avoided if it's only being used to destroy; where the waves of life keep throwing us down on old shores laced with boulders and sharp edges. This is a brokenness that comes when the world wins and ashes remain. But the brokenness Jesus guides us towards, is something to be embraced. It's a revelation of being able to see what in us needs to go, what needs to grow, and what needs to change. It's a realization of our inability and His ability which compels us to bend our knees. We see the need to lower our center of gravity; allowing ourselves, our will, our attitude, our my-way-mentality to be broken and washed away. After the work of this kind of brokenness is complete, we find ourselves standing in a new place. A place we thought we could only arrive at if "they" or "it" changed. Instead, we find the thing that needed to change, was something in us.

Now, perhaps "they" are a serious issue, a real problem, a troublesome thing to endure. No doubt there are those grievous people and painful situations that cause much angst in our lives. Certainly change is needed in them as well. But just as we have no power over the wave… we know, we have no power to change them.

Keeping our focus set on them, will rob us two-fold. We'll never see the good possibilities of bending our knees and increasing Christ-in-me; we'll never know what life could have been like after the wave-line was broken. The answer is not found in running from the waves. The answer is found in overcoming them by facing them wisely.

Brokenness.

Life is a constant remodeling, taking us from what was to new places of what can be. In order to get there, we must be willing to let the One who made us, carry us through the waves. And He can only do that when we bend our knees and lower ourselves in His hands.

He will deal with those who wrong us. He knows, He sees, He will deal with them. And a fearsome dealing it might be. (Makes me cringe to think of it, it compels me to pray for them.) But never forget, He's also watching to see how we respond to the wave-lines in life. Do we lean into Him, bend our knees and lower ourselves as He increases in us? Or do we rigidly fight the impacts of life and struggle in the surf after being knocked down again?

"For the eyes of the LORD run to and fro throughout the whole earth, to show himself strong in the behalf of them whose heart is perfect

toward Him." 2 Chronicles 16:9 KJV

In my kindergarten way of thinking this verse through, this I know to be solid-rock truth…

I can not even begin to have a "heart perfect toward Him" if I have not become practiced in bending my knees, lowering myself, and facing the waves of life. Letting the waves flow over me in such a way that what needed to be removed inside me is washed away and my eyes are found set like flint on Him.

Oh Lord, help her (the many "hers" and the many "hims" too).

Oh Lord, help me.

Oh Lord, help us all.

Wash us again and again.

Hold us steady in the waves Daddy-GOD.

We trust Your dealings with us on the path of brokenness. You can take our rough selves and find the diamond inside.

The world's dealings with us brings a brokenness that takes our stone-selves and pummels us into sand, where little if anything remains.

There are two kinds of brokenness, one destroys while the other "makes things new." We choose You and Your way, Father. Don't let us miss seeing what You see, when You look at us.

finding a new way in an old wave

ELEVEN

joy is a choice

Long ago someone boldly said to me they believed love was a choice, and I cringed a bit. His wife had confessed her unfaithfulness in their marriage; even admitting she had been with other men while carrying their unborn child. What a challenging thing for a husband to face. But his response, "love is a choice, and I will not let her choice alter mine… I choose to love."

It was such a profound moment. It shifted something important inside of me.

It is true, completely and unavoidably true. Love is a choice. We choose to love or we choose not to love. It's not their fault if we don't love them, and it's not to their credit if we do. It's all on us, our choice.

The same is true with joy. Too often we get caught up in the whirl of circumstances and stress, letting them dictate to us how we should feel. And some days can take our breath away, in not-good-ways. But, we *always* hold the key to *how* we will choose to respond. No one else holds our key. Do we forget that God in Heaven smiles with delight and nods His great head when we choose to lift our eyes above the world-mess-stress? Do we remember we are dearly loved by Him and *He is the one who is above all things?*

He can take what was intended for harm and use it for good.
He holds the earth on its axis and the stars in the universe.
He saves the world through a baby.
He saves our souls through the shed blood of His Son.

Joy immeasurable is ours because He lives, we're saved, we have a home, the King is our Daddy.

Joy is a choice.

We can get distracted and deceived to the point that we even forget it's an option on the buffet He prepares daily for our consumption. That's the game plan of the enemy, to keep us from even remembering, joy is an option we can choose anywhere, anytime.

One way to keep our hearts and minds better able to remember what's on the buffet is Philippians 4:8, "Whatever is true, whatever is noble, whatever is right, whatever is pure, whatever is lovely, whatever is admirable—if anything is excellent or praiseworthy—think on such things." Then the Word says, "…and the God of peace will be with you."

Peace and joy hold hands, they are tight with one another. So for joy to be chosen, we must manage where we allow our thoughts to dwell. We must grab hold of what's good and go with it. There is always a good to grab hold of, we might have to look for it, but there is always a good option.
Joy is a choice.

Today, I'm actively choosing to set the stage for joy, for the goodness of the Lord to be seen center stage. Joy can come when I:

> Redirect my thoughts from what has grabbed my attention, and choose to guide my thoughts to where they need to be.

> Notice the flower, the cloud, feel the wind, hear the bird-song.

> Light the candle before I pick up His Word in the dark hours of morning.

> Become captivated by the giggles of a child – thanking God for the good people caring for her.

> Hear my husband's snores as if their reminders that again tonight he chose me to rest beside.

Reframe the actions of the rude driver, instead choosing to consider they might be rushing to the hospital and need my prayers or they might be rushing to a toilet because they have diarrhea.

Linger long enough to see the kindness between two aged-people, holding hands as they walk, smiling as they've chosen to wait for each other.

Push through doubt, and choose to memorize the verse that helps us. Letting our mind go to that verse, wherever we are, because we're choosing those words instead of...

Say no to the couch/tv/phone/computer and yes to conversation that lets the people around me know... I see them, I choose them.

The list is infinite. All the ways we can choose specs of joy instead of robotic responses to life that might very well leave us feeling drained and tired. Joy has the essence of living intentionally, not reacting wearily. When we take the wrong turn and allow our joy to be connected to another person or place or circumstance, we make it really easy for the enemy of our Lord to pull the rug out from under our feet. Because no person, place, or situation can bear that load. They're not built for that purpose, it's not their responsibility. When Jesus said, "It is finished" on the cross, He was breathing out the option of joy onto any who would be willing to see it, and grab hold. But first we must see HIM. Joy comes from Him.

Ben Carson's mother once told him, given his good mind and good God, that if he (Ben) was not wildly successful it would be all his fault. (Paraphrased a bit but that was the charge she gave him.) I have learned and applied this same way of thinking to the "choice for joy". Remembering all that has been done for me, and all the options before me, if I do not choose to live-with-joy, it will be all my fault. There may be days of tears (there will be), but the flowers will still bloom, the stars will still shine. At the end of the day, what I choose is mine.

But what of those who suffer intensely? Those trapped in places of horrific pain and injustice. What of the sick who agonize with gripping, shooting, breath-taking pain? Am I supposing that joy could still be a choice for them? It's in those very arenas that knees begin to tremble and the questions will try and wipe the Holy verses out of our head. The verses that keep the belt of Truth buckled. If those verses can be overwhelmed in the midst of suffering, then joy can float down the rushing river like a life-boat cut loose from its ship.

Those are perilous, ominous waters to be adrift in.

So, let's be brave and look into those places where darkness crashes in and birds might stop singing. I think of Daniel. He was a real man. He wasn't just a long-ago-character in a story.

He was a stellar person on all sides. Even though he had been kidnapped from his childhood home, he still worked to always do the right thing and press himself to excellence. He worshiped God, served the king, and wisdom was his running-mate. But there came the day when he found himself in a den o lions, because he wouldn't succumb to a wrongly placed ruling. Was it possible Daniel allowed joy to stay inside him as he descended those steps into the growling pit?

Or what of the day he watched his three closest friends, those he had been kidnapped with and had served beside for years, being wrongfully thrown into a fiery furnace? Could joy have been present as Shadrach, Meshach, and Abednego stepped into the flames that incinerated the guards holding the door open for them?

Joy might not always show itself on the outside of a person, but it's the presence of joy on the inside that lends great strength and endurance to our steadfast resolve. Not joy in the wrongful thing that is happening, but a joy that is above the circumstance. A joy that whispers into the marrow of bones, *God is over this, God is with me, God is not defeated, God IS my good Shepherd, yes, though I'm walking through a dark valley, I will not be afraid, for God is with me, His rod and staff surround me...* keeping my eyes fixed on Him, He will finish this in His way. Joy comes (bubbles up to the outside of us) in the morning after the long night of steadfast trust. Joy is not the same thing as carefree happiness. Joy has the aroma of powerful faith.

So yes, Daniel had joy coursing through his veins as he descended into the growling den, because he knew his God was with him. And whatever the outcome, he knew God would be in charge. The three in the furnace stepped forward bravely, and joy was present in their resolve, because they knew God was about to be seen by all. At the very least they knew He was with them. Imagine the joy that rose to the surface and shined in their faces as they stepped back out of that furnace knowing everyone present had witnessed the greatness of their God. Joy was present.

Corrie is in the middle, Betsie on the left. Nollie, was also a sister, but was released early on from the concentration camp. Image from Dreaming Beneath the Spires.

Betsie, the much loved sister of Corrie Ten Boom, carried a sparkling kind of joy inside her that even though her circumstances were all-wrong, she was all-right on the inside. She died in a concentration camp, her sister witnessed her passing, but for the rest of

Corrie's life, she told the stories of joy-found in dark places. Forgive-ness-given to the undeserving. Peace in the midst of war

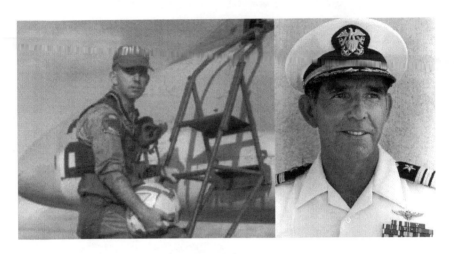

God bless Captain Jerry Coffee and all those who have suffered wrongfully while serving our country. Images supplied by Jerry Coffee.

A dear friend of mine, Captain Jerry Coffee, was held as a prisoner of war for many years. He was tortured and starved and faced many horrifying moments. Yet, he was not destroyed because he worked to keep his personal, internal (that place where no guard could reach) focus on the knowing that God was with him. He knew he was not forgotten. His testimony is powerful. Was joy with him in those dark cells? He says it was; not on the outside like a bubbling brook, but on the inside like an artesian well of promise. Joy is available when Jesus is present. Evil can not destroy it, unless we choose to allow it to do so.

Joy is a choice.

Few of us will face days of dark prison cells and concentration camps. Those are places where heroes carry joy and hope, and the rest of us watch in awe, inspired. But if joy can walk into a lions' den with Daniel, and joy can be the sparkle in a dying woman's eye, the smile on her lips at Ravensbruck concentration camp, then joy is an unstoppable force if we choose to let it live inside us.

Before Betsie died, she whispered to her sister Corrie, "There is no pit so deep, that He [God] is not deeper still." Those words could only be spoken by a woman who knew what the deep pits looked like, and found "the joy of the Lord is my strength" there.

Joy is a choice.

joy is a choice

TWELVE

behind the veil

Leaning toward Steve I said, "Goodness, it is scary." He nodded in agreement. Then as I stepped up to the guard to be scanned, she said, "You are scared? Why are you scared?" Shocked that she had heard me, I replied, "No I'm not scared, I only spoke to my husband about something that is scary."

The female guard looked me in the eye and said, "I know, and yes it is." She felt the same way I did, she understood.

We had been driving most of the day, headed north. Stopping to buy some groceries, we approached the entrance of a store just as a young woman stepped in front of me to get a cart before entering. She was not rude, no offense was taken. But it was her clothing that caught my attention and gave me pause.

She was wearing a full hijab, with a niqab, (where a small slit allows only the eyes to show). I've grown accustomed to seeing them here and there, but usually they are in full black. Her's was different.

It's still hard to believe I live so far from my homeland. But, I do, it is real, and daily my Abba stretches me to know more of Him, His ways, His plans. I no longer allow myself the indulgence of seeing things with my own eyes only. There's just so much more to be seen, understood, and done. Looking with my eyes alone would only limit me from seeing the real reason I'm breathing. There's more, there's always more. And the more Abba wants for His kids is not purchased with coins, instead it's found in obedience to whatever He is saying in the moments of any day.

Finished with the guard's scans, assured we carried no weapons, she smiled warmly as we entered the store. The fully-robed lady walked in front of us, and I noticed how everyone stared at her. She did draw attention to herself, but even from behind I sensed she did not want to be noticed. Some might think me silly, but another thing I have learned living in this country, is when in doubt----- it is time to pray. And honestly, I am in doubt so many times every day. Doubt of what someone is about to do, how the police are about to behave, where the crazy matatu drivers are going when they fly past us on the dirt side of the roadway. The doubt goes on and on.

I grew up where there was order, rules, and for the most part people followed those rules. If they didn't, they eventually ended up in jail.

But that is not the case here. There are rules, yes, but they are viewed as suggestions not requirements, unless of course the random police officer decides to enforce them. All this to say, it is always wise to pray... always. So we spend much of our time praying. It feels completely normal to us now. The crazy swirl of piki drivers, noisy loudspeakers, guards with guns, a riot of colors, and languages from 120 different dialects all within this one wonderful country of Kenya, doubt prevails... so must prayers. For sure, I love this country and its people, but it keeps me ever on my toes, no scratch that, it keeps me on my knees.

So as we walked down the first aisle and I noticed her shrinking shoulders responding to the ever-watchful-eyes of everyone she met, I prayed. I'm not trying to sound all holy and perfect when I say that I prayed. Please don't read it in that way. Instead, it was a prayer asking for protection, and an asking for her. I needed her to not do anything to harm anyone. But I could not ignore that she needed someone, anyone, please s-o-m-e-o-n-e pray for her.

If I believe my Abba Father is who He says He is (and I do), then more than anyone, I know the depth of her intense need for Him. Imagine it, she does not know the One who made her, she knows nothing of His love for her, she eeks through her days dry on the inside because she has not one drop of living water flowing through her parched soul. It hurts to see her with those eyes. But hey, why am I getting all prayerful and deep in the middle of the market? I'm there to buy onions, chicken, and yogurt, right?

Still, I prayed, "Father God, you see her, you know her, help her please... and as for us, no harm is allowed to come near us in the Name of Jesus. I'm covered and cared for by the One who is above all things... no weapon formed against us will prosper... Father help her..." As I said amen, she went straight and I turned right. It was over. Now, where do they keep the creamer I like in my tea?

Steve went one way, I went another. We Americans, we like to be efficient with our time. Our plan, we'd be in and out in less than 5 minutes. But two minutes later as I headed towards the yogurt cooler, guess who was standing near the cheeses? Reaching for the yogurt, she spoke to me. She said, "Could I please speak to you?" Within 2 seconds I had 10 solid emotions rush through me. The afraid-woman would pretend I hadn't heard her, ignore her, and walk away quickly. *But is that why I'm breathing?*

The defensive-woman would level her with a hard glance and walk away. But that's not who I am.

The unsure-woman would respond with trembling hands and her doubt would be smelled by all. Nope.

But the woman who knows who she belongs to and why she is breathing again today, knows. Buying yogurt isn't what matters, people matter.

So I paused for a breath prayer (i'm not kidding about praying all the time). Looked at her and said, "What did you say?"

"Could I please speak to you?"

"Certainly." *Lord, fill this space.*

I prepared myself for what I suspected she might want to say to me. Had she heard my words at the entrance speaking of how "scary it was"... had she known I was speaking of her clothing and how it covered everything but her hands and eyes? Was she about to confront me? *Lord, fill this space.*

I stepped a bit closer, so I could understand her timid voice. *Lord, fill this space between us.* And she said, "I am the oldest of seven children. We live with my grandmother. My parents both died in a car accident in 2008, my grandmother has cared for us since that time. She is now very old and very sick. Caring for the family has fallen to me, and I need a job please, I will do whatever is needed. I can cook, clean, it's only that I need a job." *Lord, help me help her.*

I shared with her briefly that we already have a dear lady who cares for our home, so no job was available. But I pressed ahead quickly to say, "The only thing I can do for you is pray for you, that God will make a way for a good job to come." By now, she was looking me in the eyes, and giving me the unspoken permission to look into her eyes. Much is said when eyes meet.

She responded and said, "Please do pray for me, since your God is my God, and he will hear your prayers." *Lord, give me your words, you know what she really needs.*

Ever so carefully, as gently as is ever possible, I said, "Thank you for letting me pray for you, but you must know, my God is Jehovah. And by the way you are dressed shall I guess that your god is allah?" She nodded. "But still, may I pray to my God for you?"

The look in her eyes, if only words could match the depth, she knew she needed more than just a job. She knew. She looked around cautiously and said, "Yes, please, perhaps He will hear you and help me."

I asked her name, she softly gave it. I called her by name and said, "For sure my God will hear a prayer concerning you, for whether you know Him or not, He knows you and He loves you. So I will pray for you by name as I go, but may I pray for you right now so you can hear what I will ask on your behalf?" She visibly shrank.

Her eyes darted about as if enemies lurked in bushes near by (as if we weren't in the freezer section). She said, "You mean here, you are asking to pray here?"

"Yes, you see my God is with me wherever I am. He never leaves me, He is everywhere and He always cares."

Again, those eyes. When all you can see of a person is their eyes, those eyes must be carefully looked into. There is no tilt of the lips that can be assessed, no shrugging of the shoulders can be seen, and no smirking face can be detected. Only the eyes can speak when words are measured and all else is hidden.

I called her by name again and said, "I will pray with my eyes open, and even looking at you. No one will know we are praying, only you and I and the God who is a Father." Her eyes watered, she shifted her face-cover, then ever so softly said, "Please."

And so in the frozen food section of a public market, I carried her name to the One who loves her. No veil can stop His great love-longing for her soul. We prayed, I spoke, she remained silent, and there was kindness in her trapped brown eyes.

Who was watching her? Was anyone watching her? Why was she so afraid? Yet, she had the courage to allow me to pray for her in public.

Fear. It is the enemy. Fear drives people to do horrendous things to other people all because they are afraid. They might think they are killing for other reasons, but i've grown to understand, even the terrorists are killing because of fear. They are afraid of their god's disapproval. They are afraid of what their comrades might think of them. They are afraid of being killed themselves. Two months ago we sat and talked long with two young men who grew up muslim, but converted to Christianity during their early twenties. Now they run for their lives as even their own family members search for them, to kill them, all in reverence to their god. These young men explained to us how you are trapped in that religion, and if you try and break free from it, you will suffer. One of them had been persecuted so harshly for his Christian beliefs, that when he refused to renounce Jesus, he was pushed from a four story high window. His stomach burst on impact, spilling his intestines out onto the ground. His last words to his attackers were, "You can not kill me even if you push me, Jesus will save me, or He will take me home. But you, you are not able to end me." They pushed. He fell. He burst open. He lived. As for those who pushed him, two have died since that time. The third is losing his mind and hides in his home, too afraid to be seen. Why? Because he saw Jesus save the life of the one he pushed. They knew. Jehovah is the One true God.

The lady in the market, who allowed me to pray for her, she too knows there is something more. She is trapped behind the veil... she carries an aching soul inside. A soul that Jehovah loves.

My life rarely has space to read what social media conveys. I miss most of the whirl; the words, the rants, the trending fads, the accusations and declarations. Still I know that often times harsh lines are drawn by some who hate this group or criticize that group. But as for me, my Abba reminded me as I walked out of the market that day,

"Don't be afraid, don't let the outside cause you to miss the inside that I see. Just be where I guide you to be, and speak what I guide you to say, and I will do the rest."

We are not in this world to win. We are not here to argue a point and come out on top. We are not here to dominate and rule over others. We are not here to be afraid. If we call Abba our Father, we are here to love Him and love others, and maybe we will grow in our ability to live out the truth that love actually covers over a multitude of sins. Love covers all. Love drives out fear. Love wins.

When you see the veil covering the face,
pray for the soul it is trying to hide.

behind the veil

THIRTEEN

was she found with her hands wide open?

I was alone, but not really. All around me couples walked together or people walked their dogs or groups whizzed by on their bikes. But nothing was breathing beside me. We can feel alone when we are the only one using the air around us.

So I walked long. Sand shifted under my treads, but it held fast, no sinking today. The greatness of the Atlantic to my left, a row of beach houses to my right, the setting sun before me, and all the air one girl could need around me. I talked to the One who is always in those silent, air-filled places and I listened more.

Just days before I'd shared this same stretch of sandy beach with girlfriends all around. We'd biked miles together, giggling like girls, nothing to do but ride. Laughing, lovely, vibrant ladies. Prayer warriors they are, fierce on the battlefield when arrows are flying. Peaceful joys in my life. They represent a great army of others. But we women don't usually think of ourselves as warriors do we?

We give birth, nurse life, tend wounds, and love deep. We cook dinner, read stories, cuddle cryers, and scrub away the dirt of life. We teach others what we've learned, and then let go of them so they can enjoy all they know.

Our very bodies are allowed to produce life, feed it, hold it and grow it. Then release it… and we do.

Any woman who can rise to that order is a lovely, soft, effective warrior – she can cook dinner while she's sharpening her sword. Her arsenal is found tucked between thin pages. She doesn't need guns or knives, bullets or arrows. She clings to the sword her Father said she could use.

These were my thoughts as I walked the shoreline.

Lost in thought and prayer and positioning myself to be *still* and *listen* for His more, I meandered alone between the incoming tide and the ribbon of water still lingering from morning's high tide. A visual of my aloneness with my Lord, water shielded me on both sides, the world could not come too near.

All that surrounded me had been authored by the One who was with me. One can feel like royalty in those places. Trees blocked the view of houses in the distance. No boats could be found on the water. I was truly alone in the middle of His Stuff. And the waters rolled in slowly, closing more and more off from me.

Ahead the tide had finally broken over the sandy belt I walked on, and the fresh ocean waters began renewing the stale waters of the trapped tide pools. My pathway closed. A perfect visual of our lives.

I pressed on until my toe could touch the last dry ripple of sandy beach before the incoming tide covered it over. Turning quickly then I changed course, heading back where I had just come from. Where I had been walking, the place I had thought was my way, closed before me and would no longer allow me safe passage. Increasing my pace, I walked with purpose, not wanting the waters to catch me. But I looked behind me just in time to see the waves sweep over the place where I had been. If I had stubbornly remained there, I would have been in trouble. The waters came rushing in as if they were on assignment and they brought rip tides with them, their current was fierce.

What a picture of my life...

My path had seemed right for all those years, and for all those years it had been. Then, the tide changed, the path began to close. God was insistent on showing me the purpose He created me for, He would not let me miss the clarity of His call. Many have asked me, "How do you know for sure when God is calling you?" This walk on the beach is a visual picture of the answer to that question.

God doesn't carelessly let us "miss" what He is calling us to do. He doesn't play charades with us. He doesn't give us clues and hope we can guess what He's saying, He makes it clear. Undeniably clear. Moses couldn't say the bush was not burning. Jonah couldn't say the fish was not real. God makes it clear.

There are great mysteries that surround God's ways — His ways are not our ways and they never will be. He is God, we are not. We never will be, never could be, never should try to be. It's a big movement in this broken world now, people thinking they are their own god... but they aren't. They'll realize it too, when the only faithful One remains, and He reaches out His great hand to them. Oh, He is good.

God's clarity in our lives is not a mystery. I use to think it was, I was wrong. He opened the Red Sea for the Israelites to pass through, and He closed it on those who pursued them. He put a pillar of fire by night and a cloud by day to guide them through the desert. God is clear in His communications to His kids. However, He does sometimes wait until we are ready to actually listen before He will speak. He chooses when He speaks, and we must wait until He does. Patience, it grows in those waiting fields.

So how can we know when God is guiding us this way or that way? How can we make sense of it when the course of our life seems to change right before our eyes?

We must be willing to pause. Pause long enough for the dust to settle, be still, ask Him, and wait. We must be willing to wait on the Lord. Just as He has been willing to wait on us. The problem is not that God no longer speaks, the problem is that we don't take the needed time to listen.

When we don't pause and respect that God is God and He will speak when He knows we are ready, we try and press the matter, we want to move ahead and make something happen. Then we find ourselves in the middle of swirling tidal waters pressing all around us with swift currents.

We thought we should...
but then we realized...
and now I see that...
and we are forced to a place of stillness that doesn't feel good.
And we cry out, "Where are you God?!"
We blame Him for where we are, when where we are was not His doing.

My feet were set on a good path back on Mockingbird Road. I loved that path, it was sweet and simple and all I had dreamed of for our growing old days. The front porch swing was set in place for our old age years. But slowly, ever so slowly, like advancing tide waters, that life seemed to close off from me. My eyes could see that the way ahead was no longer ahead of me if I remained where I had always been. So I stopped. We paused long. We asked. All the while the

127

waters kept closing in on our plans for our future.

And He answered. Then we knew.

We could ignore His answer and press ahead with our plans or we could change our course and obey. The first option would have brought tide waters swirling around us, for the Creator of the universe will not be ignored easily. And the second, would break us of ourselves and fill us with more of Him. There's a sweetness in that filling.

Perhaps it's what we are actually trying to get when we over buy, over eat, over plan, over control, over build, over work, over speak, over perform. We know there is *more*, but we get confused when trying to face the reality that the more we crave is found in the laying down of ourselves and the taking up of HIM. *"He must increase, I must decrease"* is how John puts it. (3:30)

But as for me and my Steve, we turned and obeyed and a new path opened before us. Wisdom says, "don't look back, keep pressing on toward the goal you are called to." But, I confess, i've looked back in my nostalgia. Just as I looked back to see the tidal waters swirling over the sandy shore.

This trip home has forced me to walk the same pathways I use to walk before, but the tidal waters have changed the way they feel under my feet. And if I linger too long, my feet will get wet.

How frightening it would be to try and force my feet back on the old familiar pathway. His mighty waters would surely wash me completely away.

Walking back on the shore line, the air around me seemed electric. There was an eagerness to walk in the way that had opened up for me. A silent pressing came from behind. And joy, real joy was present. She *whispered*, "Just look how much your Father loves you, He gives you a place to walk where the waters can not come near you." There is joy and peace in obeying. But as we obey, we can not fool ourselves into thinking we can have it our way. We can't author a spec of it. Welcome to the wall where too many children fall.

We want to have at least a degree of what we want. We might be willing to give up some of what we want — our plans, our dreams, our goals, our desires. But when it comes to laying it all down, we shrink at the thought of having no control, no say, no input, no power. The definition of surrender is, "to abandon oneself entirely," "to give in to," "to give up or hand over." And when Jesus died on that cross, his hand was open. He surrendered all.

HE the God of the universe
SURRENDERED handed over
ALL His life.

When God calls us to the more He created us for, we must surrender before we can fully obey. That's the wall. The waves come in on our plans, they wash away the spaces we would have filled if we had controlled them. They clear the way for another to walk there, as they also change the course of our safe passage.

Coming home has shown me much. My old pathway has washed away. There is a new one in its place, and I know I didn't build it. My family is still my family, and they still love me sweetly. But they don't need me the way I use to think they did. God provides. My friends are still my friends, the ones that remained faithful still walk beside me even though the course of the pathway has changed completely. It's not the path that holds us steady, it's the heart. My Father is still here too, and there, and everywhere. He's bigger and better and stronger and more faithful than my old path could have ever completely seen.

I reveled in the realization of it all as the waters closed in behind me and the waves sang steadily beside me. I was alone... but not really.

Then as I watched the sun fading and turned to leave the beach, an old horse-shoe-crab shell caught my eye. Something whispered in my soul, calling me to pause and listen. I knelt down beside the old shell and it came flooding into my heart...

"Someday you'll be just like me, you'll die too. All you do now will be added to the great efforts of the many who have obeyed the One who

made us all. There will come a day when you won't be able to walk any path, not even the path He made you for. So choose carefully now, walk the right path while you can. Your days are numbered, they were before you were born. So your last one is already known in the Heavenlies. It will come and you'll be done. Your ride will end, you will come to the day when you'll have your last chance to obey, and it will be then that you'll be more thankful than ever, that you did. You chose the right path.

"And then, you'll be still... and wait... to go home. And whether you walked perfectly won't matter a smidgen. If you pleased others or disappointed them, won't matter a mite. The topic of conversation when you open your eyes above will be, 'where was she found walking?' 'Did she stay true to the course?' 'Did she surrender and obey?' 'Was she found in the place He made her for?' 'Were her hands open?'"

I sat by the old shell of the silent horse-shoe crab and heard the laughter of my girlfriends from the day before. I imagined the chubby feet of the three little ones I have loved and released running on sandy beaches between their daddy and me. I longed for the man my soul fits perfectly beside. And I looked at my feet.

"Oh Lord... do what you must, but don't let my skin covered bones get in the way. Place me soundly where You choose. Use me up just like this old shell here. Let's get the most out of this little vapor that I am. Thank you for grace. Thank you for your patient mercies every morning. May I be found walking and loving and serving and living on the path of your

choosing. When you give me that last chance at obedience, leaving it all on the path, i'll finally come home with hands well practiced in being open."

FOURTEEN

fishing for life

He said, "They are fishing for life."

It felt profound. It had the ring of remarkable. It was the way he said it mixed with the look on his face. He was acquainted with living, we could sense it by the way he did it in front of us.

Our boat had glided across the waters of Lake Baringo pausing to catch glimpses of kingfishers, fish eagles, hornbills, and rainbow malachites. We met Susan, the Nile crocodile that would come to his whistle but not linger as a pet would. We left the 6 foot croc as he said, "We'll go buy fish and return to feed her. She'll love it." We road a distance further on the beautifully wild lake as he explained to us the names and characteristics of the mountain ranges on either side of us. We were riding through the deeper parts of the Great Rift

Valley in this part of Kenya. And he said, "Millions of years from now, this great valley will open itself up and separate these mountains from those and the sea will flow through it." Pointing to the peaks on either side of us. He lived in one of the most spectacular places in the world...and he knew it. We were quiet as he spoke of what he knew so well. Teaching us what we did not know, his eyes glimmered, as he shared pieces of his world with us.

The boat driver slowed our speed as we approached the fishermen sitting on reed grass-beds floating in the deep aqua water. As we drew nearer we could see they sat on partially submerged boat-like floats made from balsa trees. Poles of spongy, lightweight wood lashed together. Their paddles were made from tire treads cut into small, oval shaped pieces they would hold in their hands and use like flippers. All day these fishermen would sit on the floating wood boat with legs dangling in the water. A simple pole made from a long thin stick held the line with one hook tied to its end. A large African termite met its end on the hook being dipped into the water where the grass-bed was separated a bit. Like Huckleberry Fin on the mighty Mississippi, these fishermen sat patiently dipping their hooks into the water. There was a peace around them. Three men and a young boy, they fished in silence, each movement slow. And it was here, he said, "They are fishing for life."

For us, we felt the gift of being allowed into their "world". These fishermen knew the water, the fish, and the flow of life around this lake in the Rift Valley. But they knew nothing of the world we came from. Most likely, they would not have been intrigued by it at all. When you spend your days peacefully asking the lake to surrender "life" to you so you can feed your family and provide for needs, what other world would woo them.

Daily, they fish for life.
It's been their way for decades.
It's been the way on the shores of this lake for centuries.

They would have had much to talk about with Peter and Andrew and James and John. The older man was a 21st century Zebedee, fishing with his son. As we bought 3 fish from them to give to Susan, they returned to their work, fishing for life. They were busy and content. Much could be learned in the solid simpleness around them.

Our guide was their friend. They spoke in a tongue known well to them, but still foreign to us. We couldn't grasp all they were saying to one another, but we could read their gestures and understand their eyes. They knew one another well, and they liked what they knew in each other. The boy caught a tilapia and held it up proudly to show his father. We all were blessed by the joy in his face over his success. His father had taught him the work of fishing for life, and he was getting it. And I wondered to myself...*are you one of my Father's treasures? Living an obscure life, doing the next right thing, and blessing the world around you in ways that won't show loudly but will run deeply.*

Years ago when I first came to this continent, I had been jaded by the cruelness happening to countless women and children. And that warping in my mind had caused me to wrongfully assume most men here were users and abusers. Now after living here, and hearing the many more stories, my eyes see more, and my heart is no longer dark towards them. So many good men work to care for their families in the same place where some men do not. But the good ones always rise to the top. That's one way God works. He conquers evil by growing men who persevere in the ways of Light — and some of those men, fish for life.

As we left the fishermen, my husband and I let our minds settle into those words. We spoke quietly to one another realizing the three simple words had gone deep in us both, "fishing for life".

Riding back to feed Susan, the corner of my eye caught the movements of our guide as he quickly, but silently killed each of the three fish. He noticed my awareness of his actions and slowly said, "So sorry mom, but it's what I must do for their life to pass to the croc, if I do not they will swim away too quickly and keep it for themselves." And while it was a bit disturbing to realize the fish were dying beside me, it was another chance for wisdom to teach me a fuller meaning in his words.

"It's what I must do for life to pass. If I do not they will keep it for themselves." And in the oddest way, I felt the common ground between the fish and I. Dying to self is not pleasant. In fact it's an ugly, painful process. To lay down our own life, our plans, our goals, our everything...so that it can become life in other places and for others. For the fish beside me, their life would pass on to the crocodile. For me, for you, where is our life passing on to?

Christ did it first.

He gave up His life and passed life on to those who will receive it. And in the holy process, He then calls us to lay our lives down (even while we are still breathing), so that life can flow through us to others. It's the way of the One who spoke of being born twice.

Two births, two deaths, the Holy rhythm of truly having lived.

But, we people, we work so desperately to keep our lives for ourselves don't we? Just as the fish lying in the boat bottom on Baringo. It flopped frantically trying to find a way to get back to its business of swimming. It would have kept its life for itself and swam away at the first chance offered. But the one who held it knew, the only way life could pass on was for the fish to lay its own life down. The fish did not willingly do this. It had no choice.

But we do.
We are given the choice by the One who holds us.
We can keep it all for ourselves, or...

we can choose to lay down our life,
even as we live,
so that the One who knows best can freely flow true life through us
to a dying world.

Beside the dying fish, the word was whispering.
"Seek, and you will find..."

———————

Later, we returned to the shores and plans were made for our guide
to take us on a hike at the base of the escarpment not far from our
campsite. The time was set for 4:00 in the afternoon, when the heat
of the day would begin to pass. Two hours of walking was the plan.
He overflowed with passionate words talking of scorpions, snakes,
bugs, and small animals living in the crevices of the desert terrain. "I
began watching birds when I was nine years old and have now
become an ornithologist. I am most at home with what lives in the
wild and especially with what lives on the wing." While scorpions
and snakes had not been on our list for the day, the enthusiasm in
our guide drew us, and we were eager for what he wanted to share.
After completing the plans for our evening hike, my husband shook
hands with our guide, with a tip of gratitude passing from his hand
to the one who had blessed us. He could have pocketed that 500
shillings with no one knowing the exchange had taken place. But
instead, he immediately turned and handed the tip he had received

to the young man who had driven the boat. He received, and he passed it on. And there was a brotherly love in their eyes towards one another. It's what happens when we freely give what we have freely received. Love flows.

We looked forward to walking in the wild with this good man. But sadly, that walk never took place.

Our guide had taken another couple out for a tour shortly after our return. They had wanted to explore another section of the lake where great cliffs hung over the shore. Was it planned or impulse that caused him to offer to climb and dive from the cliff to the waters? We'll never know. But, while diving from a cliff, something he had likely done hundreds of times since his childhood, the one who had spoken just hours earlier of "fishing for life", dove in, never to surface again.

His name, was Cliff.
And it was from a cliff he breathed his last.

———————————

We don't know details of his life, we were only privy to the way he lived beside us for 60 minutes. He left a family behind when he left this world. We were told his fishermen friends stopped fishing and his fellow guides shut down their businesses for the day. It hit the lake community hard when they learned of the loss of their friend. That night as we slept in our tent on the shores of the lake, with hippos passing nearby eating the grass to fill their massive stomachs, drums beat through the darkness. It was a mourning coming from the village where he had been born and had lived. The beating of the drum went long into the night. And then it stopped, just as the beating of the heart had that day.

To know we had been with him when he bought his last fish from his life-long friends and shared that last portion of life with Susan, it's not something to view lightly. There's a respect that is right when the lasts are witnessed. There will be no more "fishing for life" for our guide on the lake. It was harsh and sobering to realize a man so full of life had breathed some of his last air with us just hours before. But, it was a defining moment for us. This man had left a legacy when he shared life-giving words at the beginning of his last day.

"They are fishing for life..."

Life will end. One day we will all wake up, and not know, that day will be our last. And will we be found living and speaking and acting in a way, that when we take in that last lung-full of air, those who came near us will breathe in better ways because of the way we lived beside them? Are we purposeful in the ways we *fish for life*? Do we each realize we are fishing for something? Without a pole in our hands, each and every day, we will catch something and we will pass something on to others. Will it be *life*? Or will it be *death* that's been seasoned with negativity, sarcasm, selfishness, greed?

Are we likened to a fish that's found its way back out of the boat, flopping under protest until we finally found the waters again? Swimming away as quickly as we can, refusing to "die to ourselves so that others might live?" There's no hook in these words. Just a sharing of the right questions that rolled through my mind as wisdom whispered on the shores that day.

The men on lake Baringo are literally fishing for fish. But even in that common task, they view it differently. They are not simply looking for a fish at the end of their lines. They are more accurately looking for life.

The thing they *catch* will give *life*.
And so what of us?

FIFTEEN

elephants and a boy, salt and light

He was standing between bushes on the side of the mud road. It would be better described as a narrow mud trail. His clothes, old and frayed, were almost the same color as his skin, like perfect milk chocolate. His smile. It glowed. Tiny and barefooted, he stood there alone, but he knew how to welcome someone.

He waved loudly, I waved back and smiled, trying to match the glowing smile on his tiny face. But then I noticed the twitch of his eyes. His whole forehead jerked as muscles in his eyelids moved in abnormal ways. My mother-heart jumped, but then we were past him, and I whispered to Abba.

We were on our way to speak at a Pastor's Conference. Several dozen men were expecting us; we had been asked to encourage them on unity and reconciliation. We were almost there, the Pastors were gathering, but we were "watching" for the arrival of the Holy Spirit. For in truth, we wake daily knowing, only what Abba says through us will be worth hearing. We had prayed and read and prepared ourselves as best we could, but we live with the keen understanding, we are clay vessels. Vessels that are only valuable because of what we hold inside.

So we look for the daily refilling, we ask for the overflow, we watch for the Holy One to pour Himself through. We were eager for what He would give, He knows what is needed, and He watches for which mouths will open for His Words. After all, how could we possibly know what another stands needing to hear? We can not know what Abba is doing in the life of another, but we can open our mouths to let His Life and Truth and Light flow. Amazingly, we so often do not even know what was said that helped them, even though we witness the flow. For it's one of the wonderful mysteries, He is God among us. He ministering and delivering what is needed, if we remain obedient to just show up.

We drove on through the mud trail and finally arrived at the church. Children were the first to greet us – it's almost always that way here. Ladies waved from a distance, but children were all around. Barefoot, beautiful, glowing in the morning light, they watched after each other and reached with eager timidity to shake our hands and greet us with, "How are you?" (said with the most lovely accent and always inflection on the "you"). And then sliding into the mix of them, was the little guy from the bushes. His smile captivated. All their smiles do. Unhindered by the mud between their toes or the tears in the clothes, they were open and excited. They had someone to welcome, they shined with something so much more lovely than gold.

As we shook hands and giggled together, we were thankful for the gentle way God was easing our nerves with His little ones. We never stand to teach with a gloating confidence, we are always willing, but always a bit unnerved. It takes obedience and attention to not allow human flesh to hinder the flow of God. Any pitcher meant to carry good, clean water needs to be scrubbed clean first. The children were ministering to us with their eager goodness. So often the smallest among us do the most good.

But I noticed the eye spasms of the first little boy. They had increased. Between each muscle twitch his eyes would almost close. It was disturbing to watch. The mother in me wanted to load him up and take him to the nearest doctor. But it is most important to show respect for the adults around him first, to see what others have already done.

As we met with the church ladies and sipped Kenyan tea before beginning the first session, the children lingered near, including the little boy with the twitching eyes. I learned that just the day before a medical clinic had taken place at this very church. Hundreds had come and been cared for by a team of Kenyan doctors and nurses.

An American team had raised funds for the clinic and provided meds to be administered. Ministry at its best, in my opinion, many working together for the good of those in need. Unity that blesses outward. So I asked if the little fellow had been seen by the doctors, did they know what was wrong with his eyes? The kind lady said he probably had not been seen.

The doctors only attended to those who stood in line to see them, and there had been a long line all day. But why had no one stood in line with him I asked. I thought of the man who had sat beside the pool at Bethesda year after year, never able to get into the healing waters because no one had helped him. She replied, "We should have thought of this and made sure he was seen, but you see, his mother left him long ago and his father is a picky-picky driver who is gone from sun-up to sun-down. So there was no one to wait with him in line."

She was remorseful I could tell. But I quickly reminded myself she had organized a clinic where hundreds of people had received care. Attention was needed for the boy, but words of appreciation and encouragement were in order for her.

She called a friend over, a pastor in the area who knew of the boy's situation. He explained that months ago the boy's father had taken him to a doctor nearby and had learned there was some sort of neurological disorder developing in the boy that did not allow proper filter of sunlight. He could see better at night than he could in the day. He wasn't in pain, he was just unable to hold his eyes open in the light of day. And I reminded myself, he is a boy whose father is working long hours to try and provide. He has a father who faithfully returns to him each night. May God bless that father. I asked who watched over him during the day while his father worked, she waved her arm wide and said, "All the mothers surrounding him".

The Pastors were gathering, it was time to focus on why we had come. But the little guy tugged at my heart.

Inside the little tin church there were no lights. Doors opened wide let in the needed sunlight. Many men sat in a large circle and worship began. Breezes wafted through as bird songs dominated the loud voices of worship around us. Just outside the open doors, a water spout stood, giving clean water from a deep bore-hole. Children lined up with their assortment of plastic jugs, waiting their turn to gather the needed water for the day. These little ones did not have to walk miles for water. They only had to walk to the church each day... such a beautiful thought in so many ways. And while they waited in line, they danced to the worship. The children teach us, if we are willing to learn.

Introductions were made, we began to share what God had placed on our hearts, the air inside the stick-pole, tin covered church was wonderfully sweet. We all sensed Abba's nearness. Then as we spoke I noticed movement just inside the doorway. Steve was talking so I was allowed the time to look more closely, and warmth flooded me as I realized it was the little boy with the twitching eyes. He noticed my eyes on him, he smiled so sweetly as his eyes held steady. No spasms or squinting. He sat as peaceful as a lamb, completely still, looking around, smiling.

We talked for the full length of the time requested of us, almost four hours. And for much of that time the little guy sat inside the nice shaded church. Other children carried water and later played in the distance. But this little guy… he stayed in the shaded places inside the church. While his father transports riders on his motor-bike all day, this son finds his solace in the shaded, breezy church. And I wondered, whose eyes are healthier?

In this world we want eyes that can see clearly in the light of day and we understand we should not be able to see well in the darkness. It's what we expect, what our eyes were "designed" to do, right? But as I watched the little boy who found rest in the shaded church, who danced to the worship and sat quietly as we spoke… I pondered it all. To be able to see clearly, even in the "darkness", it can be done when there is Light.

Bats and roaches and leopards come out at night. Darkness is equated to the evil one's arena in the scriptures. But where do we sometimes find those who are hurting the most in this world?

Here in Kenya, we have been cautioned by Kenyans that we should be where we need to be by nightfall. An occasional drive home from a rare dinner out is ok, but it should not be often. Here on the "dark continent" (as it is often referred to) it is wise to be safely tucked indoors before darkness comes.

Dark places can be very dangerous. But, this little boy spoke to my soul, without saying a word. *The light is wonderful, but it can be blinding for those in the darkness.* Bright light is hard on eyes that have only ever known darkness. So as I live out the Light that I so dearly love and cling to, may I be ever so patient and gracious when I encounter those whose eyes are stung at their first glimpses of the Light. Without words, a little boy with damaged eyes, can teach me.

In caves not far from our home, elephants journey deep into the catacombs searching for salt deposits. They make this journey at night, in the darkness. During the light of day they graze on vegetation that is life-giving but it lacks the salt they need. So at night they take the journey into pitch black caves, scrape the walls with their tusks and eat the salt they find there. How interesting, they go searching for salt in the dark...

I wonder how many living in the light of day are still hungry for more Salt... too many times God's good news is watered down, and the saltiness is too. Or could it be at times there are too many other "spices" offered on the table, when truly only good *Salt* is needed.

I remember my Savior was often found in "dark" places, shining the Light and sharing *Salt*. It can make living on this dark continent taste right to this southern born day-light-loving girl.

Matthew 5: 13 - 16
"You are the salt of the earth. But if the salt loses its saltiness, how can it be made salty again? It is no longer good for anything, except to be thrown out and trampled underfoot.

"You are the light of the world. A town built on a hill cannot be hidden. Neither do people light a lamp and put it under a bowl. Instead they put it on its stand, and it gives light to everyone in the house. In the same way, let your light shine before others, that they may see your good deeds and glorify your Father in heaven."

SIXTEEN

oh the places He is found

It says, *"All humanity finds shelter in the shadow of your wings."* Right there in front of my eyes, David said it, wrote it down, in another age, so long ago. But the words still speak into today. The Creator cares about and offers shelter to all humanity, and not just in a mansion on a secluded hillside, but also in a shack in the bowels of the earth. The Word says all humanity finds shelter in the shadow of His wings. And the shadow of His wing is found right up under His shoulder, up close, beside Him.

Oh the places He can be found...

"Come pray for a little girl please, she is very sick, and she needs many prayers." Those words carried our feet on the packed-earth pathway that weaves between mud slathered walls holding up rusty roofs. A tangle of twine tied from this one to that one held dripping laundry, washed in muddy waters from the stream at the bottom of the hill. Those tight, closed in places where living souls are trying to breathe and live in the midst of stagnant air and too much evil. We walked quickly, as no good would come from pausing beside the overly friendly men sitting beside the bowl of fresh cooked brew. Here, you walk with purpose, with intent. We arrived at the doorway and stepped inside, leaving the bright light of day and entering into darkness. Eyes must be given time to adjust, if I don't give them time, I'll stumble in the darkness.

As eyes adjust, so does my soul. An adjusting soul doesn't need time as much as it needs the whispering of prayers. God's Word tells us to *"Guard our hearts above all else, for everything you do flows from it."* (Proverbs 4:23) So when entering "dark places", it is right to be diligent to put a guard over our hearts. Prayers are right when we step from light to dark.

Some might say, "we shouldn't go there, we should protect ourselves best by not going to the dark places!" But my soul has heard His voice speak clearly in my heart… *why have you been given such a great Light if you are not willing to carry it into the darkness?*

Two steps from the blue sky canopy, the rusty tin holds many shadows. But the sounds inside the tiny hut are sweet. A mama speaking softly in Swahili and a child making childlike sounds and my eyes adjust. And slowly by slowly I begin to see. Within the four-wall room that is their home, a mother holds her five year old daughter. The treasure in her arms wears not a stitch of clothing but the mother holds her close. You can feel the love in the room. Her daughter's head is dramatically dis-proportionate to her body, the little girl's head is larger than her own mother's. She struggles to hold it up, but she works hard to do so because she has a smile to share. And her smile is a carrier of intense J-O-Y.

Joy.

This naked child suffering from an accumulation of fluid on her brain (hydrocephalus), is a giver of joy... and the story told by her mother's eyes needs no language of the ear... this child is loved. In this slum area tucked in Africa where much is needed... my senses focus in on one thing, love.

My human eyes go to war with my heart. My eyes want to shoot arrows of "this is so wrong" but my heart rests in an other-worldly place. Responding to my humanness, my heart whispers solidly, "she is loved…she is loved…she is loved…she smiles with joy. She knows what it is to be deeply loved. Look at her mother's eyes, she is dearly loved…"

One of the things I have learned here in Kenya is that a child with a birth defect is rarely abused by those who do evil things (molesters, abusers, rapist, etc.) because they are "afraid" of catching the "curse" they believe she carries. They usually will not even touch the child.

So this treasured one, is not molested by wicked hands, and that is a great merciful blanket that surrounds her unclothed shoulders.

Her mother holds her as we talk, a translator helps me understand what the mother shares. Little Mary is her third child, two others are older. Mary's father is a good man who sells fruit and vegetables in town to provide for his family. The mother gathers wood in the nearby forest, she then sells to her elderly neighbors. She says of her husband, "He is a good man..." Those are golden words to hear from the mouth of a woman in a slum in Africa. Few women can speak those words in these places.

Time slows down. In a world that struggles with the rush of busy, here, in these moments, it slows down. Time slows down for little ones like Mary and the kind mother who holds her. The outside world is shut off from these places. No electricity lines in these alleyways, no television shows invade here, no internet, no emails, no social media presenting its fabricated appearances. Life is raw and basic. Food and shelter and water take priority. There is little time for other things chased after by the masses who live beyond the horizon.

We've been asked to come and pray. We've not been asked to come and fix or change or do. We've been asked to pray. Again, the priority is solid and clear. This mother does not know what is wrong with her much-loved child. But she DOES KNOW that praying for her beautiful daughter is what is needed. Prayer... simple, earnest, heart-felt prayer.

We pray and little Mary rolls her head from side to side. But as I pray, she blesses me with rays of JOY as she works hard to hold her head steady long enough to be sure I see-her-smile-of joy. It's all she has to give and she works hard to give it… and I know Jesus is present. The mother wiped eyes that grew wet as we called out to the One she knows loves her daughter too.

Simple faith in a far from perfect place.
Pure love in a hard and dirty world.
Complete joy in a child's eyes who knows nothing beyond the place where she lives. And I sit, amazed beyond belief at the magnitude of the wave that rolls through me.

As I leave their hut, I try and help the two dear friends who are with me in their processing of what they just saw and how they are internally responding to it. We usually respond internally before we take action externally (we should), so healthy internal processing can lead to better external thoughts/actions. I know they are stunned – shocked — overwhelmed perhaps (likely).

Less than a week prior they were doing life in America, today they met "life" in a completely different setting. Every sense is challenged and all those questions impact the heart before dripping down into the soul. And the processing of it is an important step, for the soul to be impacted in God-honoring ways.

The enemy of our souls is ever watchful and eager to make us view things in distorted ways. He's always looking to make God appear a liar (that hasn't changed since Gen. 3: 1-5).

So as my guests and I walked and talked, I encouraged them to try and see little Mary's world from her eyes. She is loved. She is cared for by the tender, gentle hands of a mother and father, which is rare in this world. She is fed, and held, and washed, and safe. She actually has more joy and contentment that many children who live in fine places. We look at her and see neediness… SHE DOES NOT. And we must be careful. We must seek God diligently before we let her see "our" eyes and impose on her a look of pity. Pity would be a mystery to her. For she lives wrapped in joy and love.

Oh it's a hard moment indeed, but it's part of the *"I must decrease and He must increase"* that's found in John 3:30. We must learn that our Abba does great things in hard places. He doesn't have to have polished, pretty, well-decorated rooms to work His great miracles. And in this world, isn't the presence of complete joy and love a miracle? Our minds might want to demand that healing would be the right miracle... but would we overlook the miracle of joy and love in the midst of sickness?

I've learned many hard lessons living so far from all that was familiar and comfortable. I've sat long and silently (imagine that miracle in itself) and looked up. And i've embraced the suffering that happened at the Cross – where the blood of the Innocent One flowed down on the souls of the guilty masses, and the miracle of salvation was birthed through unimaginable pain. And i've learned... that my Abba can work so beautifully in places where we weaker ones shrink back. He's not afraid of suffering. He's not afraid of pain. He knows exactly what to do with it. He works miracles in the places we hesitate to touch.

So in the processing with my dear guests, I asked them, "do you think we should immediately cast a net to the many who love us and love God – and raise funds to have a needed surgery to place a shunt in little Mary's body? Do you think the risk of invading her body through surgery done here (not in America, but here, where surgery looks very different) and with recovery time required, in the place she lives now? Do you think that is for sure the right thing for her? Do you think we should "rescue" her from her home, the only place she has ever known, and bring her into our home, for a safe recovery?

Bearing in mind her mother and father will not be able to be beside her because they will have to remain in their hut so squatters don't take it from them. And what do you think will happen to her little heart, her mind, her soul, if she endures the surgery, recovers in our home, then goes back to her home wondering why?

Why is her home so different, why does water not flow threw a pipe, why does light not hang from the ceiling, why...why...why? And in those moments do we really think the enemy of her soul will miss the chance to drain her of the valueable love and joy she now glimmers with?

She will always need follow up surgeries...
She will always need a clean place to live...
She will always need good medical care...
For her to live long, she will need these things.

Life is valuable. This I learned many years ago as a child. But living long is not the most important thing about life. The value of life is found in the way it is lived. What we do with it, how we share it, if we love others with it. Do you know anyone who lives their life for themselves? What they want? How they can get what they want? Who they can use to get what they want? Distracted... from the needs of others because of the many distractions they surround themselves with… Are they living well? It might possibly look like they are, if we just view the "outside" of them.

If we just look at the outside of little Mary's life, we could wrongly judge it and say, she needs to be rescued from the one room shack in the middle of a slum. But if we pause long enough to feel the joy-of-the-Lord in the radiance of her smile, we can more accurately see the good life in her. Perhaps she was placed exactly where she is, by the hand of a God, who because of His great love, also placed His Son on the cross. Abba can work miracles in desperately hard places. And we can feel the intense weakness of ourselves in those same hard places. Doesn't He remind in His word that *"in our weakness, He is strong."* I asked my young visitors to let God guide them carefully as they processed little Mary's situation. Not to view it through "American", "Western-world", "save-the-world" thinking. But instead to allow themselves to face their helplessness and in that moment choose to see God's able-ness to do all that is needed regarding His precious little Mary. Then in those moments, in clos-et-prayer-with-Him, ask Him if He would have them do anything according to His good plans for her.

I did the same. I prayed fervently in the same way. Oh it can feel so wrong to not jump in with everything we've got, thinking, "this is wrong and I must do something." But in the quietness of "being still and knowing that He is God," peace flows strong to trust Him and believe, He knows what He is doing and I do not.

Perhaps you're reading these words (if you've made it this far) and you might be thinking, "this woman is a nut!" I'll laugh with you there and say, I might just be. But all I can do is learn what my Abba is teaching me, and trust what He is doing. And when He says jump in, may my feet clear the ground at "j". But when He says, "hold steady I'm doing a work that doesn't need your hands," may I sit still and pray. It's a part of *"He must increase..."*

The hard truth is this... precious smiling Mary will likely not live to the fullness of 80 years. She will most likely succumb to an illness sooner rather than later. But the life she is living right now, in the little hut of her mother and father who love and care for her, is rich.

She sparkles with joy. She rests in love. She is content with the sounds of her mother and father around her. She brings Light into a dark place. She proves, things do not have to be perfect in order for them to be good. She *preaches* the good words, *"under His wing, refuge is found."* His wing is not limited in where it can reach.

Mary will someday leave this earth, just as we all will.

But I am most certain of this one thing, when her little brown feet step into her Maker's Heaven, her head will not falter when that sparkling crown is placed on it. And she will not need help when she lifts it from her normal-sized brow and places it at the feet of the One she is well acquainted with. Her days here may be shortened only to allow them to be increased in a land where there is no suffering, where the lion lays beside the lamb, and no disease or sickness is found.

Guide us Lord, help us Father to see things more with Your eyes and realize how very needy we all are for more of You and Your ways.

And Lord, thank you for the joy you have placed inside of little Mary. Help her Lord to shine Your love in a dark place. Bless her momma and daddy, give them all they need, fill their hut with your greatness, and if you choose to ask us to action on your behalf regarding Mary, we are most willing. We trust You and what You are doing more than we trust ourselves and what we would do. So you guide and we will follow. Oh Lord, thank you for being God. Thank you for little Mary.

Thank you for little Joseph, that precious little baby you put in front of me just four days ago. With his ulcered skin sores and whimpering attempts to scratch them. Thank you that with him you whispered so surely, "this one... this one... get him the help he needs." And now already, the meds are working and he is being healed.

Oh the places You are found...

"God will never forget the needy; the hope of the afflicted will never perish." Psalm 9:18

oh the places He is found

SEVENTEEN

between a rock & a holy place

The toughest professors in my college courses never came close to teaching me at the deep levels of cognitive and spiritual development surrounding me these days. Truly, my rate of growth only reflects the harsh reality that there was so much I did not know. I've never thought of myself as "highly intelligent". But I never realized "just how little I knew" until stepping into the arenas where logic doesn't compute and no amount of "want to, try to, hope to, maybe I can if I work hard enough" will make an ounce of difference. When in one place, there are innocent little ones being broken. Physically struggling to get through another day of hunger and pain. While just a few lines of latitude and longitude traveled reveal a similar innocence being emotionally ruined by lavish unnecessaries piled around them. But always, in the back of my mind, I remember the Garden of Eden.

Eden was God's plan. His gift. In Eden, no one person would have had too much while another suffered without.

These reflections are not meant to present some magnificent theological finding. They're just the ponderings of a daughter. One who is growing.

The scriptures roll through my mind, "the Lord gives and the Lord takes away, blessed be the name of the Lord." And I say, "amen." The Lord is blessed, He is holy and just and loving and merciful. But what of His children? How often are we acting out *the will of The Lord* in our day to day living? How much do I act out *the will* of the Lord around me?

The struggle… do I give food to the street children who are ever near me these days? I buy a bag of oranges to share with the two boys with scarred feet and torn clothes. And I look at the bag in my hands. And I struggle – missing Eden. Some would actually criticize saying, "don't give them any food, it only encourages them to stay begging on the street." I get that point. Others would say, "what would Jesus do? He would surely give them food." I get that point too. Some would say, "just get out of there, come back home to America, where you can avoid the tension, and eat your oranges in peace." *Oh Father…*

I even say to myself, "what are you thinking Donna? you're so far away from your own children, don't you know you are risking never being near them again with this obedience?" We aren't suppose to admit things like that are we? But...

Yesterday a pregnant, filthy street woman who looked to be 90 years old came to me as I bought onions at the market. *Oh Father!* Her hand is out, she needs help! She carries a little one inside. She's also "mindless" as my Kenyan friends would describe it. *Oh Abba.* How did her life come to this? Logic says, "Donna, you can not give her what she needs... you can help her for the next few minutes... but in the end, you can not 'fix' her life." This logic is accurate. But... what about the words, "do unto others as you would have them do unto you."? In all this tension, this terrible tension, my smallness is painfully clear. A tiny bush on the side of the escarpment bordering the Great Rift Valley.

Many would say, "the problems are just too great, it's too over-whelming, I'll look away or better yet I'll stay far from it. I'll just keep living my life, and I'll pray for them..." Sometimes it feels like the only possible response to the great need in this world.

But then God plucks a daughter from the peaceful place found at the easier lines of longitude and latitude. Then He places her in the middle of where His heart is, and she stops to hear HIS VOICE.

She realizes she knows too little.

She cringes at the contrast of the two worlds. And He grows her in

His ways. "He must increase... I must decrease" (John 3:30) becomes a heartbeat, no longer just inked words on neat white paper.

She realizes she's a pebble with many rough edges. She's tucked in with all the other pebbles at the bottom of the stream. The flood waters come rushing over her. She can hardly breathe. Other pebbles surround her, she can endure if they can, right? But then the water somehow plucks her up from the sandy bottom. She misses the comfort of the spot she had always occupied in the middle of those who held her securely in her place. Still the rushing waters have swept her away. She crashes into bigger, unrelenting boulders that line the boundaries of the water's edge.

Every collision knocks off a sharp edge on her, an edge that had been unseen by her until the moment of impact. But when the chiseling blow comes, she knows sharpness had been there all along, and it needed to go for her journey down the stream to flow more gently. It's a painful journey down the waterway, but it's so very necessary. She realizes, while tucked into the sand, the rough edges had not been so evident. The sand could cover. Only the part that was exposed, had felt the rushing waters; and those waters had nicely smoothed the portion that had felt their constant flow. But only when the current had pulled her away did the jagged, sharp, far-from-smooth sides show. The steady stream didn't seem to notice or care, but she did. She knew. She had thought she was smooth... but now her jagged edges protruded and collided. She was being changed, transformed, altered, awakened.

For as she found herself carried by the rushing waters, she was seeing things she'd never seen before. She was impacted by boulders she'd only heard of. In truth, she had been afraid of the thought of such huge boulders and hoped she might never have to encounter them. Tucked safely in her stream-bottom-sand-bed, she had felt certain she would be safe from them. And yet, she was now learning. The giants didn't break her to pieces, they were only allowed to chip off tiny pieces, she had hoped would never be seen. She was a pebble being tossed about at the will of the rushing stream. She had no control over her course. Helpless. But.... not hopeless.

She knew as she encountered another giant boulder, she could do nothing to alter it. But if she just let the waters carry her through, the boulder would impact her and she would be changed. What needed to go would be chipped away. If her already smoothed side was the surface that hit the giant rock, she would slide off easily, nothing would chip away. Only the jagged edges would chip away when they hit the giant hard places.

The One who made the stream. The One who plucked her from her safe, sandy bed. The One who was over the boulders and set her course for the journey through them. That One would someday gather her up at the end of her journey, and hold her in His great hands. And He would hopefully be able to say, "oh little one, it's been a hard journey hasn't it? You've been tossed about, but look at you now. You're smooth in my hands. There is nothing about you now that would prick another. There's no side of you now that has not been touched and shaped. The boulders were cruel. Not even I wish for the boulders to be so hard. But since they have chosen to be that way, I have chosen to use them in ways that will bring about my good purposes. For you see, I've been steadily at work to help you. You're heart had cried out to me, you wanted more of Me. You wanted to bless others, not cut them with your sharp edges. So the work began. And little one, all along the way, you thought you were having no impact on the giant, hard, unrelenting boulders. But you did. Look back. My rushing waters that carried you through have been working on smoothing those hard places in this world. You alone didn't change them. But the combination of you, along with many others in My waters, made a difference.

"Some of the boulders are now many tiny pebbles rushing down the same stream you've just traveled. And some of the cruel boulders are even now being slowly worn down and weakened. Little stone in my hands, I will use you and the many like you, to transform even the hardest places. You will never understand the hard places. Your mind is not equipped to do so. But I do. And I'm at work.

"I, God, know the pregnant homeless lady who ripped at your heart yesterday. I know her intimately. You can't change her any more than you could change the boulder beside the stream. But I, God, I will continue to flood my waters over her. She will not have one day that I, God, am not willing to draw near her and smooth away all that is rough and wrong. She might not feel like she has a choice. But remember my Word… if she will turn to me, she will find me.

"You, just be my pebble. Allow me to toss you according to my good will, for your course is not hap-hazard. I chart each turn and curve. Be aware of all that you do not 'know' and the starkness of all that is wrong in this fallen world. Face the moments of newness that over-whelm you and make you feel your intense inability and weakness. Just be a pebble in those moments and allow Me, the One who is not weak, the One who loves you dearly, the One who is not over-whelmed. Allow ME to carry you through. I will accomplish what needs to be accomplished.

"You just attend to releasing yourself into the rushing waters, let the rough edges be removed, and in the end, I will then allow you to see all that 'I' accomplished during your journey."

between a rock & a holy place

a little about the author

Donna Taylor is a wife, mother, grandmother and as she puts it, a life-long learner. She was born and raised in Georgia, her parents Kathryn and Donald Glover were the first to instill in their daughter an appreciation for learning and doing much with what was given. Following in her father's footsteps, Donna became a teacher shortly after marrying her Steve.

For the next fourteen years she taught elementary school aged children, raised three children, stood beside her husband through good and tough times, planted flowers in her favorite flower beds and began free-lance writing on the side.

After fourteen years, Donna realized that God was calling her away from her dream of being a teacher and moving her towards a life serving others in a different way. She became a trip coordinator for those wishing to serve on missions trips in Africa. The following years would be filled with trips back and forth with her family serving in different parts of Africa and then always returning back to their beautiful home in Georgia where she continued to care for her flowers in her favorite flower beds.

As time passed and once all three of their children had graduated high school, God moved in big ways again and made it evident to both Steve and Donna that it was time to serve in different ways yet again. They sold everything and what they could not sell they gave away. She said goodbye to her flower beds as they moved away from their home of thirty years and stepped into a new life living in Africa. Despite how painful it was for them to move, God had made it clear that they were to teach Godly Principles of Marriage while mentoring and encouraging couples to bless each other, honor God and care for their children and homes.

Between culture shock and missing their loved ones back home, the move to Africa brought with it much heartache and a great deal of learning and growing both spiritually and mentally. Donna found that one of the best ways to cope with the transition was to pour her feelings out with pen and paper. Words would help her process the new things she was learning, the new emotions she was feeling and the new adventures she never thought she would be on.

She started a blog known as *Reaching for the Robe* and after a while she wrote her first book, *Dandelion*. After an unexpected positive response from both the blog and the book, Donna was encouraged to continue writing. The book you have just read is a compilation of blog posts, some old and some new but all with valuable lessons to be learned. If you enjoyed this and would like to read more from this author, you will find the first chapter of *Dandelion* on the following pages. You can find the full copy, hardback and Kindle versions, on Amazon.

And in case you were wondering, Donna has begun planting flowers in new flower beds. She realized that it doesn't matter where flowers bloom, for with the right amount of love and care,

they will be beautiful.

Chapter One

THE GARDEN

What Happened Then Still Happens Now

The Shattering...

It was a perfect evening as we peacefully walked through historic streets of an old seaport town. The night air held that wonderful mixture of warm ocean smells and cool coastal breezes. Sea gulls sang overhead, competing with the old-salt crooner outside the corner coffee shop two blocks away. It was one of those rare moments when everyone was kind, no one was in need, the leaves in the trees brushed one another in musical ways, and tears had been given the night off. Even the bench beneath us, with its weathered and worn curves, welcomed us to rest where many others had found solace for countless decades. Ice cream cones in hand, we watched as families walked by under twinkling lights strung in ancient oak trees. Peace. Laughter. Joy. Contentment. And then that eerie sound of crackling breakage... the sound that precedes the shattering of a beautiful glass window. But it was not broken glass that sliced open the picturesque evening. It was her voice, her words. This young woman, likely in her 30s, passed in front of us completely unaware of the joy that gave way in order to accommodate her hasty pace. She turned boldly to her husband, never batting an eye, and said, "Well, if you'd just give me what I want, we wouldn't have any problems." And the street froze. It was only a split second, but for sure the guitarist and the gull held their voices still as the slight glimmer of salty tears began to build in the eyes of the man walking behind her.

The struggle was on.

The man was whipped up one side and down the other, not by leather, but worse, by words. The gleam in her eye boldly declared that she knew she was winning and whatever trinket she fancied was soon to be bagged.

We cringed so acutely, we wondered why neither of them noticed our reactions. It was not as it should have been—for either of them. It was not as it should be in any marriage. But the struggle comes and goes and, in its wake, so many are left wondering, *Why even try?*

Our guess is that the man gave her what she wanted and for a few hours (or maybe just a few minutes), they appeared to have no problems, just as she had said, "If you'll just give me what I want... " But when the next "I want" rolled around, a new problem would appear, at least until he gave in again. What a painful, sad way to live.

Demand and Supply

A business thrives based on its ability to manage the flow between supply and demand. Fortune 500 companies are perfect examples; they find ways to supply products in high demand, and the rest is history. But in a home, in a marriage, those words too often get flipped into *demand and supply*. Left unchecked, they become a death sentence for relationships.

Neither the wife nor the husband on the quaint street corner was living the way God intended. They were enduring, struggling, getting their way, or falling in defeat. But the gift of relationship, joy beside each other, companionship with peace . . . none of these were present. And we winced over the sad looks on both their faces. Getting her way was only a temporary ointment for the some-thing's-not-right feeling she had deep inside her.

It showed in her eyes. And giving her what she wanted in order to keep her "happy" was another mauling of his manliness. He felt it fading away. His broad shoulders and thick wallet made no differ-ence. He knew that she ruled him and he died a little inside.

But what do you do with it even if you're brave enough to admit it? You fight sometimes. You try and stand up for what you think is right. But in the end, the winner wins and somehow you both lose.

At other times, you give in quickly and hope that someday it will magically get better and you'll begin to actually enjoy life together... every day... not just when one is getting his or her way.

We can change the setting, recast the main characters, alter the story line just a tad, and *BAM*, there it is again—hurting couples who maybe started out really liking each other, perhaps even loving each other, but after a few months (or years), one begins getting, the other keeps giving. They struggle over it; get over it; but somehow it seems to grow in the mildewed closets of their hearts. Left unchecked, it brings them to an end ... either the end of themselves or the end of their home. Either way, death is sure to come calling even though no one has stopped breathing.

Do We Really Need?

There's a serious wrong on both their parts and many books on marital conflict and resolutions can help us work through the issues that need to be addressed between wounded couples. But this book is not a book just about marriage; it's a book meant to share a truth that was left behind long ago. Did it get buried in that first garden? It seems it may have.

This book will often refer to relational dynamics in marriage, but it is not a book specifically for marriage. Instead, it focuses predominantly on one-half of the marriage, the wife. What does she really bring to the marriage, the home, the relationship? Even more important is the question: *What did God intend her to bring?*

She was meant for so much more than we have been able to see as spoken by the One who made her. God's plan for his daughters has been overlooked for so long, some say it is obsolete in today's world. We feel differently. We believe, instead, that understanding those God-breathed words over his girls is perhaps needed more than ever today. Until we understand it, we can't live it. And we can't understand it until someone shares it. So here's to sharing for the hope of authentic understanding, so that heaven's purpose in creating the woman can be lived out in homes unfettered by the tangled weeds that grow in uncared-for gardens.

Let's dig deep into the reasons every wife needs to be seen and heard and cared for, because she has more than we've ever fully realized within her, waiting to be discovered. But if she's not cared for, if she doesn't understand her intended value, her unmet needs may trickle out in wrong ways, ways that end up tearing her home apart rather than holding it together.

Some of you may have flinched at the words "every wife needs," because for centuries, women have been wounded and some have declared that women don't need anything from men. But declaring that wives don't need . . . well, those are wounded-warrior words. For in truth, we were all made with a heart-shaped need for relationships.

Once Upon a Time, Long, Long Ago . . .
In the beginning, God created him; God created her; God created

them. It was the response to a need that brought about the birth pangs of their creation. And from that day until this, there have been beautiful moments intertwined with moments of hurt. Sometimes the hurt is a shallow scraping, but often it cuts clear to the bone. It was never meant to be this way.

To begin rightly, we should lay a foundation. Let's revisit the garden. After all, it's the historical birthplace of that first woman. Most have heard the story of her creation, but in case you haven't, take a minute to read it for yourself. Her name was Eve and her beginning is found in Genesis 2:18–25. Some of us have heard the story since we were children. But when we hear something many times over, we often begin to think we know it completely. Today, let's take a long, indubitable look at the garden again and see the deeper truths that have for ages been lost somewhere between the serpent and the sin.

Creation 101 tells us that God the Creator made the heavens and the earth, light and dark, and separated the waters from both the sky and the lands. He made vegetation to grow out of the land and he separated day from night. Then came the creatures for the seas and birds for the sky.

Imagine it.

Five days of work and at the end of each day, the words "It is good." Then day six brings lots of work creating cows, rhinos, raccoons, giraffes, lions, and tigers, and bears... oh my! And God saw that it was good. Next up, and still during the waning hours of day six, God created his image-bearer—man. Does it spin anyone else around in your seat that after that amazing day of work, God's words do not reach a mountaintop crescendo of GOOD? Instead, the Creator looks at the last thing he has made, the man, and speaks the words, "It is not good for the man to be alone" (Gen. 2:18).

My farmer grandfather had a wonderful saying and I still hear his voice. When he wanted to sit with a thought for an extended amount of time, he would say, "Let's wallow in it." And usually after sitting still beside him as he wallowed over the matter, he would have something wonderfully wise to say. He would have allowed himself the time to "figure it out" or at least to see it from a different, perhaps more meaningful, point of view.

There was a peace about sitting beside my grandfather when he "wallowed" over something. There wasn't a striving or squirming; there was instead a desire to see it anew. No matter how old we get, our minds will remain youthful if we wisely try to see things in new ways. And while he only had a third-grade education, he became a very successful farmer, likely the result of lots of good wallowing.

So rather than rush through that creation scene, let's wallow in it a bit...

The Creator knew the plans and purposes he had in forming the woman. He saw the need in the heart of the man; he was alone in this perfect garden. God knew this first woman could perfectly fill the aloneness. She was created to be that just-right fit for the man. God wanted it to be clear why he was making this gift called wo-man. No matter how the world has defined her role, God, the One who made her, wanted it to be clear WHY he was creating her. God spoke of her identity when he named her.

From His Side

Since God is God, and he is omniscient, he knew humankind would be prone to warp and twist his reason for creating this gift. So he was meticulous as he created and named her. He did not make her in the same way he made Adam. Genesis 2:7 tells us that Adam was formed from the dust of the ground and God breathed into his nostrils and he became a living being.

The Hebrew word for man, *adam*, sounds like and may be related to the Hebrew word for ground, *adamah*. But Genesis 2:21–22 says, "God caused the man to fall into a deep sleep and while he was sleeping, God took one of the man's ribs and closed up the place with flesh. Then the Lord God made a woman from the rib he had taken out of the man, and he brought her to the man."

Adam came from the dust of the ground. Eve came from Adam's side. Do you think it possible that Adam saw the poetry of the gift? She was from him, bone and flesh; she was a part of him. She was not of the ground; she was of him, created for him from his side.

Thousands of years later, Jesus' side would be pierced on the cross. In the garden, Adam's side was opened as well.

But Adam did not experience any pain in that first surgery. God put him to sleep in order to take Eve's beginnings from his side. Isn't it worth pondering that the Savior (the new Adam) experienced excruciating pain when his side was opened as he willingly gave his life to pay for the sins of the first Adam, as well as the sins of all humankind (Romans 5:12–17).

The One Who Made Her Called Her...

Maybe you've heard it before, but it's worth revisiting. The bone and flesh (v. 23) were not taken from Adam's head, implying she was above him, and they were not taken from his foot, implying she was beneath him. God chose to take the bone from Adam's side, signifying she was made to be beside him.

God did not allow Adam to watch her creation take place. It was a private matter between God and this gift to Adam. She was his daughter. Father's have special places in their hearts for their daughters. The Father feels deeply for his daughters as well.

Before all this took place, before she was formed and given as a gift to Adam, God had already called her by name. God did not give her the name Eve. Adam named the woman Eve (Gen. 3:20). It was before she was even created and in response to his own words, "It is not good for the man to be alone" that God gave a precise name to what he would create to alleviate Adam's aloneness.

He used two important words to describe her purpose beside Adam. The words would speak of her identity, not her name. Our Bibles today do not use those original Hebrew words spoken by God. Today's translations use words like "helper," "helpmate suitable," and "companion suitable." But when God first said it was not good for man to be alone, he used two Hebrew words to describe what was needed for Adam. God said he would make an "*ezer kenegdo*." An *ezer*, a helper. A *kenegdo*, one who is strong, even powerful, who is opposite of the man, who has a warrior-like way willing to stand beside the man and against evil.

Made for More

God's *ezer kenegdo* is one who will help the man stand against evil. Pause a moment here and think of the wives you know. Do they stand beside their husbands for the purpose of helping him stand against evil... evil working to wound their family... evil trying to damage their relationship? Can you see the strength of those women and the way their courage is being used to benefit their homes?

And think of other homes where you see the wife standing in opposition to her husband. Is it possible she is doing so because he is (knowingly or unknowingly) allowing some wrong to happen in their home? In their marriage? And, if so, in those moments of opposition, is she actually standing against her husband or is she standing against the thing that left undefeated will destroy the home she longs to protect and nurture? Warrior women who are trying to fight for what is good surround us. They are trying to protect the home. But have we seen it rightly?

Some women who have lost their way use the *kenegdo* strength inside them for their own selfish gain. Do you know any women like that? Women who want what they want and they'll do whatever they need to do to get it? These women are opening the door wide for evil to attack their homes. They don't understand (or sometimes they don't care) who they are supposed to be in their homes. They are ignoring why God made them.

Remember the woman at the beginning of this chapter? Walking down the street in the quaint seaport town, she was thinking of herself, not her home or her husband, not even about what was right or wrong. She was thinking of what she wanted—*her way*. She literally wanted her husband to "just give her what she wanted" so they could then be *okay*.

It's a sad trade she was willing to make. And even sadder still is the fact that she was in no way living up to the real purpose for which she was created. She was using her strength and her warrior-like ways to manipulate her husband into letting her have her way.

She would settle for an *okay* life getting what she wanted, rather than an amazing life beside her husband helping him stand against anything that would harm their home.

To live this *ezer kenegdo* way, she wouldn't be getting what "she wanted" all the time. Rather, she would need to think about what was best for the whole of her home. She would need to ask herself, *Is this thing I want good and right or is it not good and not right for the whole of our home?*

She obviously didn't want to ask herself the challenging questions that would lead her toward making a wise decision. Instead, she wanted her husband to let her have her way and if he didn't, she would cause him trouble. That's a far cry from her call to be an *ezer kenegdo.*

The Pause, The Question

But what if, instead, she had "wallowed" in her desire for a few minutes. What if she had asked herself the right questions and allowed self-control and wisdom to guide her answers? Letting go of what she wanted for herself and looking more broadly at the big picture would have allowed wisdom to defeat selfishness, and she might not have been brawling on the sidewalk with her husband looking like a three-year-old throwing a tantrum. She could have blessed her husband with an honest conversation expressing her wants. There's nothing wrong with wanting something. It's what we do with those "wants" that determines our character. She could have allowed her husband to see her pause, question, and perhaps wallow in it a bit. She could have let him witness the process of her thinking through the rightness of her desired purchase or the realization that it was not necessary after all.

In expressing a want and then pausing, questioning, and processing long enough to choose the best outcome, respect could have grown between them. Sadly, though, the woman on the street that night was self-centered with no thought of being a "helper suitable." If she knew the real reason she was beside her husband, she might have been able to see the thunderclouds on the horizon as the MORE, the goodness of God's plans, slowly came into sight—more peace, more kindness, more self-control, more happiness—for both her husband and her. If the balance is not managed, then the scales will always tip to mean more for one and less for the other. This is not what God intended.

It sometimes feels as though we live life in our homes as if there's only a certain amount of love and goodness to give and receive. We act like goodness in marriage is little more than chocolate cake on a plate. And we better get as big a slice as we can before it runs out. Marriage is not meant to be lived looking out for number one and every man for himself. It's meant to be a place where the artesian well of God's goodness flows between two people in infinite supply. The catch, or the valve, on the artesian well, though, is directly connected to being "open" to let good flow through us for the benefit of another. When two people are willing to let good flow through them for the benefit of the other, their home thrives! Does that sound a little "over the top" to you? Like maybe I'm crazy to write such a thing in a world where divorce rates continue to climb? If so, then perhaps we think that way only because we've seen so few real-life couples loving each other this way. It's what God intended. The chocolate cake doesn't have to run out or get old and grow fuzzy-looking mold on it. An *ezer kenegdo* living out her purpose and a man beside her living out his can be where goodness multiplies and hope begins to grow for those who see it.

But if either the *ezer* or the man beside her begins to focus on getting all they can, "Me first," "What's in this for me," "You owe me," "I deserve . . ." "If you'll just let me have my way" kinds of thinking, then the scales will tilt wildly, balance will be lost, and one of them will fade away while the other indulges. And their home will feel empty (no matter its size or contents). At least shooting stars look beautiful in their quick demise. Not so for the marriage that dies from the painful imbalance preceding its slow burn and burial.

Paul speaks clearly to this imbalance in Ephesians 5:21: "Submit to one another out of reverence for Christ." She submits to him and he submits to her out of reverence for Christ.

Now, don't worry. We're not denying the clear guidance of God's Word for wives to submit to their husbands. (We spend time addressing this in Chapter 8.) But in establishing a foundation for the book, we want to remember that in order to show reverence to Christ, there should be mutual submission between a man and the gift God gives him in a wife. Those are not our words. They come from the Creator through the pen of the apostle Paul in Ephesians.

Aloneness Can Happen, Even Beside Someone.
God made Eve for Adam because it was not good for Adam to be alone. Just as Eve is the mother of all women, Adam is the father of all men. If Eve were created to solve the aloneness in Adam's life, where does that leave the downtrodden man walking the old-seaport street behind his wife that evening?

He was most certainly a man, alone.

Just as medical students spend long hours and invest countless days studying, interning, and preparing for the day they will finally perform the surgery that saves a life, so it is for the woman beside a man working to stand against anything that would bring destruction to their relationship. Medical students don't get to do whatever they want. They must do the right thing for the patient. And aren't we thankful when doctors do the right things for us?

Likewise for a wife. She can't do whatever she wants. She must do what she knows is the right thing for her home, for her husband, even for herself—the inner woman, the *ezer kenegdo* she was created to be. And everyone fortunate to live in her home, including her, will be blessed.

I've always loved this verse in Song of Solomon. It encourages and inspires me in many ways. It's life giving to know that I can emerge from the "wilderness of life" and step into a new place (out of the darkness). To successfully emerge, I must be found leaning on my beloved. Some might think the word "beloved" is referring to a man, a husband. Not me. While I love Steve dearly, and I do lean on him in some ways, this wilderness emergence will find me leaning on my first love, my Savior, the One who died for me. It is only HE who can save me in the wilderness, walking me out of darkness and allowing me to lean on him as I find the clean, clear air of a new place. No more wilderness confusion or fear. Instead, with him I find a new way, a new me, who is better able to be what he had intended all along.

The doctor goes to medical school to learn, the lawyer to law school. The woman must go to God. She must learn from the One who calls her an ezer kenegdo. What does he really mean? What does that look like in the eyes of the One who made her?

If you would like to read more, please purchase
your own copy on Amazon today under
Dandelion: A warrior beside him

Made in the USA
Columbia, SC
12 January 2019